# The Spirit of Ceramic Design

Maria Eitle-Vozar, *Card House Village*

# The Spirit of Ceramic Design

*Cultivating Creativity With Clay*

Robert Piepenburg

*For Gail . . .*

Published by Pebble Press, Inc.
1610 Longshore Drive
Ann Arbor, Michigan 48105-1678
E-mail: pebblepress@gmail.com

Publisher's Cataloging-In-Publication Data

Piepenburg, Robert.
   The spirit of ceramic design: cultivating creativity with clay / by Robert Piepenburg.
     p. cm.
   Contents: part I. Essence of design—part II. Cultivating your design aesthetic—part III. Design relationships in clay.
   ISBN 978-0-9628481-7-9 (pbk.)
   1. Design—Elements, principles. 2. Ceramics—Aesthetics. 3. Creativity—Artistic. 4. Spirituality (Human, creative, etc.) 5. Self-realization. I. Title.

Library of Congress Control Number: 2007936255

Editing: Kathy Rowenchuk
Cover art: Craig Underhill, *Group of Untitled Vessels*
Cover design: Jessica Yurasek


Printed in China

*The reach of your compassion is the reach of your art.*

JOSEPH CAMPBELL

# Contents

PART III

# Design Relationships in Clay 123

## Essential Elements of 3-D Design 124

## Organizational Principles of 3-D Design 184

# *Foreword*

This book is about the spirit of design in clay. It is an examination of how design and spirit influence creative output—how one makes it art and the other makes it meaningful.

Design and spirit are two very challenging concepts. To help reach an enhanced understanding of their importance to ceramic artists, the significance of self-love is also given a place of honored sensibility. Together, these three transformative forces form a verifiable core of what it takes to be authentically creative and to keep in sync with a host of personal possibilities.

Much of what follows is directed at uncovering underlying truths about the creative and aesthetic workings of design that inform our artmaking and engage the human spirit. Whether or not you are enriched or inspired by what you find here, there is a path with clay that is entirely yours, one that welcomes only you. In the current state of your life's unfolding may this book be one of your escorts and may it invite you to both seek and savor the nascent originality of your own design spirit.

# PART I

# Essence of Design

*Good design, like good painting, cooking,*
*architecture or whatever you like, is a*
*manifestation of the capacity of the human*
*spirit to transcend its limitations.*

GEORGE NELSON

1

# Design Defined

*Design is like gravity—the force that holds it all together.*

EDGAR WHITNEY

Everything is design. And the design within everything is an exemplification of mankind's identifiable unity with life—his creative gratitude and personal engagement with living. If that isn't enough to grab your attention let me go one step further by adding that innovative design is a human phenomenon (right up there with a few of mankind's more enduring virtues) that moves all of us through the realms of our innermost consciousness and into experience. Design is and always was an enabler and without question it can be a magical, mysterious, and compelling trigger of influence. It is therefore no coincidence that any successful design—whether it be a ceramic work of art, an Apple iPhone, a political campaign or the ambience of a Starbuck's—can drive right through reason and emotion to the core of those unspoken yet real desires of the individual.

Simply stated, design is where personal and worldly necessities intersect—a sustaining link between the facts of life and the values of life. Designs in their neverending diversity permeate every aspect of our existence. At their best they can be life affirming, serving as quasi-vehicles for sensations through which a philosophy of life might emerge. Acting as delicate motivators they can, in the words of William Blake, "Allow us to see the world in a grain of sand, and heaven in a wild flower." Designs of inspiring substance can generate emotional bonds, uncover hidden aspects of the psyche and, in practical terms, prove useful by allowing us to experience a greater sense of completeness in our lives. At their worst they can cause us to question ourselves through their inability to make our lives feel a tad more settled—or worse yet, leave us to coexist with their inadequacies.

While a precise definition of anything may be mutable, finding an acceptable definition of design might be impossible because what design is is immeasurably different to a multiplicity of disciplines—both inside and outside the field of art. The primary tenets and fundamental concepts that give guidance to design practices are, at their core, universally inherited and recognized as an essential part of human object-making. Every artifact in our environment exists as a unique and accountable expression of an individual's functional and/or aesthetic solution to a need. There is no object, no product, no structure where design isn't present. Yet design is more than these tangible things. It is process, a strategy, a plan of action; not just for our now but also for our future.

It is not my intent to put forward an all-encompassing definition of design that describes every facet of the subject. That would be far too daunting a task owing to the fact that design is applied in an infinite number of ways and in a variety of circumstances. My aim is to delineate how the process itself is both object and spirit—how a design becomes a physical entity through spiritual consciousness and how the designing process is uniquely important to the discipline of ceramics and to the medium of clay.

For the ceramist, design is an indeterminate process of visual and material problem solving with an infinite number of possible outcomes. It is a procedure for bringing imagination, observation, organization, evaluation, and resolution to clay in a way that is both personally and aesthetically satisfying. As process, designing in clay is a creative interplay between some physical and other not so physical forces that invoke a fresher vision of self and a more responsive reaction to form. For myself, some important concerns are met through my ceramic design activities. I don't simply work with clay because it works with me (although as I write this it sounds like a pretty good rationale), but rather because it provides pieces of a puzzle that both highlight and give shape to a larger picture of life.

*Art is an idea that has found its perfect visual expression. And design is the vehicle by which this expression is made possible. Art is a noun, and design is a noun and also a verb. Art is a product and design is a process. Design is the foundation of all the arts.*

PAUL RAND

In developing a definitive understanding of design it is helpful to try and comprehend the self-evident nature of art itself. It wasn't all that long ago that design was denied parity with art. Equality existed but it was seldom affirmed. Both were viewed as separate and distinct spheres of innovation. One was identified with *fine arts*, the other with *fine objects*. Painting and sculpture were held in higher esteem than the designs of furniture, buildings, textiles, or anything characterized as functional. Today the divide between the two is so indistinct that one is all but synonymous with the other. Witness

Herman Muys, *Untitled Container #32*

the fact that more people travel to Bilbao, Spain, to see the architectural design of Frank Gehry's Guggenheim Museum than to see the art inside. Or that the spectacular silhouette of the latest Ferrari evokes the sculpted contours of Michelangelo's *David*. Endless comparisons can be found, but the point to be made is that art and design are not polar opposites and that they are not so much different as alike. Any questions still remaining should fade with time as have the old divisions between *art* and *craft*. The art auction houses, museums, galleries, and collectors no longer find such distinctions all that relevant—why should ceramists still measure the integrity of their work by such criteria when they do more to inhibit creative growth than to promote it?

Sometimes our unconscious devotion to ceramics doesn't allow us to appreciate its connections to other forces. The best of ceramics reveals itself to be inclusive: a strong emergence of art, design, and craftsmanship working in partnership. While art is created in union with the spirit, it still helps to visit its conceptual birthplace for a clearer definition. One touchstone definition of art is the use of any material in the service of a personal statement, a characterization that could also apply to design. Only here the term "intention" or "purpose" might be a better substitute for "statement." Of course these designations are appreciably the same, but more importantly a definition is always second to its effect. The same holds true for the term *craft*. The word itself is often associated with skillful and experienced workmanship in a more or less traditional manner. To the ceramist the craft is the implementation: the skilled performance of quality workmanship needed to achieve resolution. As a vital component of the design process, craftsmanship brings a desired completion to the work. If the workmanship is lacking the work suffers—even if it is well designed and well conceived.

*A man who works with his hands is a laborer; a man*
*who works with his hands and his mind is a craftsman;*
*but a man who works with his hands,*
*his brain and his heart is an artist.*

ST. THOMAS AQUINAS

Art, design, and craft each play a necessary role in the creation of ceramic objects. Each has a poetic dimension that captivates us and leads us to make constructive connections between our sense of self and our impassioned drive to make things. Because designing is an intimate activity, the importance of generating our own definitions cannot be overstated if we are to be inspired by a personal sense of trust. Any collapse of self-trust leads to worry and breakdowns in creativity. Since self-expression requires a self, how we define these three aspects of artmaking is a short footstep away from how they define us and characterize our actions. As Paul Gauguin said: "The work of a man is the explanation of the man." So as an issue of individual attributes, the internalized values we live and work by need to be our own if they are to become revered and constructive. Regardless of how they're stated, our definitions differentiate us from others and restore the center of our confidence.

Art = Idea
Art is the creative concept of an inspired imagination.

Design = Development
Design is the guiding strategy of form arrangement.

Craft = Making
Craft is the quality level of workmanship in construction.

What defines a good design easily surpasses its definition. Virtually everything made by mankind is designed and could be looked upon as art as well as craft, but what gives a design value, acceptance, and appreciation is in the eye, gut, heart, and spirit of the beholder whether they be scholar, art connoisseur or idiosyncratic ceramist. Designs worthy of acclaim share many things in common. They all lift our spirits and set off a chain reaction of responses that excite, stimulate, energize, provoke, fortify, control, appease and remain etched in our minds, growing ever more memorable as our aesthetic identity matures. Good designs continually grow and mature as we do, moving beyond the dimensions of time and visual beauty towards levels of reverence. What's really enlightening about reverence is that via its virtuosity some designs acquire a mystifying ability to influence or bring about changes in opinion and conduct. Paul Woodruff, in his book *Reverence: Renewing a Forgotten Virtue*, asserts that without reverence "an instructor is not a teacher." I think the same is probably true in ceramics; that without a capacity for reverence the designer is not an artist.

It would seem that to be a really good ceramist one has to have an aptitude for managing many things simultaneously, in the same way that a truly good actor can portray many layers of human behavior concurrently. It is not uncommon to find people working in clay who are addicted to one of the three major phases of object-making at the expense of the other two. Some are attracted to mastering technique with the goal of making perfect forms. Others are drawn to the design phase and are dedicated to finding ideal ways of transforming concepts into form. And then there are those devoted to content and to the challenge of infusing the work with a sense of meaning that relates to personal experience and/or the human condition. When we fail to see these three phases as contributing to the overall wholeness of three-dimensional work, things fall apart. Each needs to be respected for the resource that it is, yet it would be a mistake not to recognize their interdependent nature as a source of aesthetic unity.

*The reason why the world lacks unity, and*

*lies broken and in heaps, is because*

*man is disunited with himself.*

RALPH WALDO EMERSON

Albert Einstein said that there are two ways to live your life. "One is as though nothing is a miracle. The other is as though everything is a miracle." In a similar but somewhat less extraordinary frame of reference there are also two principal ways to approach design. One is spiritually and the other is intellectually. The commercial design industry is product-focused and generally oriented towards the "form-follows-function" approach that embodies formal organizational qualities, qualities that are best met with the intellect. Artistic design is form-focused and may or may not have a functional requirement that contributes to its meaningful outcome. As an aesthetic response to visual relationships it relies more on the spirit than the mind for inspiration and empowerment.

*Form follows function—*

*that has been misunderstood.*

*Form and function should be one,*

*joined in a spiritual union.*

FRANK LLOYD WRIGHT

Industrial design is very pragmatic in meeting the needs of the client and the user. Its solutions converse with the mind in a real

Shozo Michikawa, *Vase Tanka*

world vocabulary of how, when, where, and at what costs. Ceramic design is more personal, and with an ongoing sense of intimacy it is visually directed at meeting the needs of its creator. I don't imagine that Peter Voulkos ever created his large stack pieces for a client with a set of exact specifications. His muscular clay pieces were about personal process and were made solely for his own gratification. If you knew him you would also know that his work embodies his spirit and that his ceramics will forever endure because his spirit resides in his creations, rendering them timeless.

There are ceramists who design and make work specifically for others, but in general they create one of a kind pieces and not production runs. It is a mistake to associate ceramic design with factory-like manufacturing even when there are subsequent expressions of multiplicity, marketing production, or profit incentives. Designs in clay, for the most part, have a primordial code: some primeval basis that is more instinctive and unconscious than reasoned out. That primal nature which is mystically vested on the fringes of human nature brings an originality and a uniqueness to each work of clay in the same way that every work of poetry is original and unique unto itself—no matter how or where it might ultimately subsist.

Ceramic designs also abide by the personal integrity of the ceramist and can be defined as conciliatory. They exist as centrifugal gifts of invention, instinctively influenced by a centripetal relationship with self. Whether they are appealing, functional or collectible isn't nearly as important as their authenticity. Authentic designs are nurtured extensions of a deeper self and within the inertia of a personally expansive relationship they are a voyage through spirit. And so the act of designing—like this book—is a spiritual voyage: a summons to enter those realms of awareness that make clay and life beautiful.

*The creation of something new*

*is not accomplished by the intellect*

*but by the play instinct acting*

*from inner necessity. The creative mind*

*plays with the objects it loves.*

CARL JUNG

An increase in awareness is not without its difficulties. Our state of awareness is not only a state of mind, it is also a unique manifestation of our spirituality, and to reduce anything to a simplistic division of dual categories (mind and spirit) is to run the risk of overlooking truth itself. As a product of both mind and spirit, a constructive design transcends materials and technique when it expresses the full measure of one's own being. But for now as we seek to uncover the full power of our design activities it helps to understand the differences between these two approaches: one that seeks the guidance of sequential reasoning, the other the governing wisdom of spirit. In comparing these two categories of design, the potential for conflict between certain sensibilities and aesthetic realities is heightened and illuminates any number of predicaments. While one is holistic and right brain oriented in its ability to relate the parts to the whole, the other is annalistic and left brain oriented in its breakdown of the whole into its parts. Both are and always will be essential to the designing process. After all, who is to say which is weightier: metaphysical vision or the concrete fact? But for our purposes this contextual dualism will pilot the way to a more comprehensive definition of design—one that will hopefully serve our needs as designers in clay.

## Design Category Characteristics

| Rational | Spiritual |
|---|---|
| Utilizes logic | Utilizes intuition |
| Thinking | Feeling |
| Mechanical | Organic |
| For public use | For private gratification |
| Mass-produced | One–of–a-kind |
| Fixed | Relative |
| Quantifiable standards | Personal standards |
| Commercial performance | Personal acceptance |
| Price | Significance |
| Function | Appearance |
| Dependent | Autonomous |
| Visible | Invisible |
| Linear | Non-sequential |
| Utilitarianism | Symbolism |
| Impassive | Empathetic |

In the world of ceramics, design is personal inspiration—be it rationally or spiritually sustained in clay. Correspondingly, our innermost quest for truth is personal motivation sustained in the world of philosophy. Both may increase over time, adding meaningful value to the practice of design.

Rollo May once posed the question: "What if imagination and art are not the frosting at all, but the fountainhead of human experience?" The designer in me thinks he intuitively understood how the creative mind keeps us full of life and on the go—continuously moving forward. The veracity of our inspirations, like the verity of our imagination, are energy forces of life. Along with our fantasies and emotions they are the raw ingredients of our humanity. Inspiration is a crucible within which all sensations are continuously mixed and remixed. A good design, like many things we value, is a heartfelt culmination of this eclectic mix of ingredients. As with life, the inspirational influences surrounding design are limitless and the scope of their understanding encompasses not one but hundreds of truths.

*In art the hand can never execute anything*
*higher than the heart can inspire.*

RALPH WALDO EMERSON

Hard to describe, awkward to·conceptualize, difficult to teach, perplexing to apply, and impractical to evaluate—these are qualities that can apply to any definition of design which in many ways is beyond explaining and understanding. Still, the inspirational influences and intuitive expressions of its elusive, enigmatic, and inscrutable nature eventually bring forth aesthetic manifestations that are every bit as real and concrete as we are. In a similar fashion, we too are indescribable. Each of us is hard put to articulate a comprehensible definition of who we are. We could put down in writing many subtle and not so subtle descriptions of self, but in truth we are invariably indescribable. Yet as the designers and fabricators of our clay work we constantly connect and communicate with our indescribable self.

As you may have come to realize, there are different ways in which to approach design: from the initial needs and desires of the individual (within the context of various times, locations, conventions, materials, and technologies); through the activities of the actual design process itself (with all of its creative options and procedures); and finally from the end result (the way in which the design enhances the work and impacts the quality of our lives and spirits). Each of these is one part of the design collective and each, complete with its own challenges, adds to design's efficacy.

Enric Mestre, *Untitled*

*Every artist dips his brush in his own soul, and*

*paints his own nature into his pictures.*

HENRY WARD BEECHER

When I'm in the presence of a good design it grabs me right away and I'm totally exhilarated. But to know exactly what defines design, let alone a good design, can leave me speculating for long moments in time. Perhaps what it all comes down to is that design is simply definition resistant. On a deeper more meaningful level we can decidedly see that it has not one but a combination of definitions—each as true as the other. Because we design for our survival (out of necessity) as well as for our desire (out of an innate quest to infuse life with transcendent value), designing can be about personal choice as much as it can be about a collective decision. It can be about engineering as well as marketing, both explicit and suggestive, driven by style and taste as well as money and passion. Ultimately it's left to each of us to form our own working understanding of what it entails and what it can offer.

True, design is hard to define. Yet we know that it begins within our subjective selves. In fact, most of what is deeply meaningful— love, beauty, art, friendship, happiness, serenity—collectively emerges from similar dimensions of experienced feelings. The authentic, the exalted, the enlightened feeling of self lives far beyond the intellect. Every design idea or design activity we choose to undertake has its true nativity within the depths of our aesthetic and spiritual identities. With that as our energy source we can give artistic shape to clay, affirmation to the human spirit, and inspiring definition to the indefinable.

David Roberts, *Eroded Vessel*

2

# Design as Language

*Great art speaks a language which every intelligent*
*person can understand.*

ROBERT MENZIES

Design is a visual language of communication and as with all languages it possesses a distinct system of symbols, signs, components,
and conventions. More importantly, however, it has its own vocabulary and although this vocabulary prevails as the universal standard
it also has many dialects. In fact, you could say that every artist who
utilizes this visual language is conversing in a different dialect.

It is in the unique nature of artmaking itself that each individual
makes distinctions between the specific characteristics of vocabulary components and applies them in a manner that is personally
expressive and meaningful to the task at hand. The screen language
of the filmmaker is highly specialized and different from the jargon

of the automotive model maker. Terms such as *camera angle*, *actor placement*, and *editing* are specific to one group and not to another. While the vocabulary components utilized by ceramists have common similarities to those used by architects or furniture designers, how they are used in relation to one another when working with clay is exclusive.

*True creativity often starts where language ends.*

ARTHUR KOESTLER

Humans create, use, and rely on a number of languages when creating their lives by design rather than by default. Languages are systems of intercommunication that help us to plan, strategize, and arrange the details of living. They allow us to articulate ourselves, correspond with others, and convey our thoughts. There are languages of social interaction, group behavior, politics, business, finance, and music, to name a few, and then there are the languages we write and speak.

When I was in Africa one of the astonishing things I discovered was that there are over a thousand languages spoken on that continent. Until then I thought the number of American Indian languages spoken in the United States was unusually high and they only add up to forty! What's even more intriguing is that many written languages have scripts and alphabets (the written components of languages) that are aesthetically engaging and visually alluring. I still remember where I was when I first became attracted to the Arabic alphabet. The twenty-eight letters and numerals (which are relatively clean and stylistically consistent) left me with such a sensory response to their restrained and sparingly abstract appearance that even today I equate it with having experienced the artistic joy of encountering the geometric simplicity of a Brancusi sculpture. Then there's my intense fascination with the compressed complexity of Chinese calligraphy. After many years of respectful wonder I still find it extremely handsome, yet excessively complicated. I'm tempted to think that at some point a formal language might be needed just to articulate the stroke order and patterning for characters containing more than fifteen elements.

*A different language is a different vision of life.*

FEDERICO FELLINI

It is within the context of languages themselves that we gain a greater understanding of design: from its human intricacies to its far-reaching effects on civilizations. Design has had a long, symbiotic relationship with language. This interdisciplinary union has been recognized for some time as having a self-sustaining voice. As language, design communicates with everyone and knows no boundaries. Pick a country, a place to visit. If you choose to make your way there you might find yourself unable to read the signs, speak the language, use the currency, comprehend the customs, but you will be able to understand and appreciate those visual factors that satisfy the personal and functional needs of its inhabitants. Nonverbal communication and interaction through the "use in common" recognition of designs in architecture, transportation, implements, and clothing make such a worldwide exchange of information possible. Typically, these widespread uses of design make it easier for us to fit in. Through the collective integration of design standards we are invited to make ourselves at home almost anywhere, not only within the context of the present but also within the past.

So much of what we know about an individual or a culture we

know through design. If, for example, we see the design of ceramist Robin Hopper's garden we know more about the sensibility of Robin Hopper. If we see the designs in Florence or Venice we know more about one of mankind's greatest advances, the Italian Renaissance. The creative spirits of Brunelleschi, Donatello, Leonardo da Vinci, Michelangelo, and Raphael survive from the fifteenth century in their inspired designs and speak to us today in a voice that will never go silent. Our contact with this historical past is made possible through the timeless voices of design. The challenge today is to stay on point, not so much by translating the design fundamentals of past masters into the current context of ceramics, but by aesthetically vocalizing them in clay with a similar sense of grandeur and artistic accomplishment. Bernard M. Baruch once acknowledged that, "The ability to express an idea is well nigh as important as the idea itself." How right he was. For we, too, are coming to the realization that the survival of our artwork depends on our design abilities.

*High thoughts must have high language.*

ARISTOPHANES

Design is the life that lies beneath that of our art. To fabricate a new clay piece is to cross a threshold of communication that leads to an environment where a visual language with a vocabulary and dialect all its own is spoken. If the language of design is spoken well, this environment is stimulating and becomes rich in every conceivable way for the individual in the ceramic arts. If not it is a place of struggle, with visual illiteracy and aesthetic poverty being the only recognizable outcomes. Silent in its lack of visual elegance and coherent relationships, it offers little hope for success and enjoys no sacred moment of transmission—no completion.

True completion of a work of art is separate from all traditional and predictable solutions and lives as a visually liberated entity unique to the speech of our own being. Its response to self is sacred in that its visual connections resonate within us to all that is real and truthful. So how do we know when each of our works is truly finished? The answer is we just know. Each of us has our own personal knowledge, our own way of knowing that a piece is done and that its design speaks in our voice.

> *Do not think so much about what one should do,*
> *but rather about what one should be. Our works do*
> *not ennoble us; but we must ennoble our works.*

MEISTER JOHANN ECKHART

During times of creativity each of us uses the language of design differently because our comprehension of the nature of design can be far removed from even our closest colleagues. Eventually we learn that for every person who believes form should follow function there is an opposing view somewhere else that form should follow feeling. How others choose to approach such things doesn't matter, for our designs are what we create with guidance from within and with each creation we add something new to our design vocabulary that helps our understanding of what we've accomplished and where our creative discourse might go next. The language of design is supposed to be the solution to many artistic problems but as a solution it should not be a disguise that conceals each and every obstacle. Not all obstructions are language related, many are self-induced and require adjustments. Whenever we make choices that don't feel right we should ask how we might change things for the better. Without

Gennady Roitich, *Container for Important Word*

Paul Davis, *Slab Form*

getting drawn into specific issues surrounding problems of personal compromise, it's important to realize that the language of design contains the spirit's vocabulary and that ceramics is a way of manifesting our spirituality in material form.

Psychologist Abraham Maslow (most noted for his theories of human needs) once stated that: "If the only tool you have is a hammer, every problem looks like a nail." Thankfully, many in the arts already have a co-creative history of self—one that reflects many valued experiences. Therefore most of us recognize the fact that we're not one-dimensional creatures, but multi-dimensional beings with interpenetrating energies—possessing not one tool but many.

To speak the language of design fluently we need to feel our wholeness and not ignore the subjective role of our individual psyche in any creative context. For me this inner rapport with self is symbolic of the clay in its most innate, unprompted, and inherently workable state vs. clay in its technically crafted and final glazed state. The natural state of clay embodies its authenticity and is comparable to how we experience ourselves through the vision and energy of our creativeness. At the same time, that creativity remains vulnerable to over-manipulation and the eccentricities of external influences. It's admittedly true that what we design designs us, but it is also true, once we've opened up to and embraced the wholeness inside us, that who we are is how we design.

*Men honor what lies within the sphere*
*of their knowledge, but do not realize*
*how dependent they are*
*on what lies beyond it.*

CHUANG TZU

As we instinctively know, we are all interdependent. We need the help and support of other people, yet that is not a justification for renouncing our uniqueness and our freedom to use the language of design as a translating force. Otherwise we're just hammers lying in a toolbox of non-creativity. By remaining connected to the true spirit of our authenticity we are open to a whole slew of creative tools that allow us to do extraordinary things with our imagination. In addition to laying claim to our true nature, we're able to transform the vocabulary of self into an unfolding language of expanded creativity.

Whenever we integrate our creative imagination with the spirit of our authenticity, a bold step is taken onto a life path that, if merged with a design path, becomes an opportunity to speak with one voice—a voice that is alive in both our artwork and our lives.

*Creativity is the power to connect the seemingly unconnected.*

WILLIAM PLOMER

The language of design is dynamic and capable of phenomenal achievements, yet at its core it consists of a set of elements and principles that are and always have been universally recognized and accepted. The primary elements of line, shape, form, space, value, color, texture, time, and light are imbued with innovative potential and are acknowledged to be the productive foundation for conceptual inventiveness. The guiding principles of balance, movement, unity, variety, pattern, emphasis, proportion, and mystery are responsible for organizing, choreographing, and skillfully recycling the functions of the primary elements. Without the controlling influence of the design principles, the separate design elements cannot operate together as an effective whole.

The signature aspect of this language is that everyone who employs it utilizes it differently. The intangibles of designing are so closely related to character, to values and attitudes like integrity and intention, that they can only be used to produce our best designs when they make sense to us on a personal level. It is a language with no dictionary or grammar to acquiesce to and this is the precise point where things get interesting, if not exciting. The fascinating thing about this language is that, in addition to its universal readability, it is also decidedly personal in how it is interpreted and spoken. Every user has the potential to speak it poetically in his or her own way.

*Let us say what we feel, and feel what we say;*
*let speech harmonize with life.*

SENECA

What's infinitely more remarkable is the burgeoning effect this language has on the world and the social order around it. If you think of design language (with its inventory of elements and principles) as being inside a very small circle that is surrounded by a slightly larger concentric circle (symbolically representing all designers) and then envision them both encircled by a third circle that is immensely larger, you will get a sense of the extent of its multidimensional influence. As a language, design is more inclusive than a vocabulary of grammatical elements and principles. It includes the creative individuals who write and speak it as well as the individuals, societies, and cultures that read and utilize it. People from various nationalities and ethnic backgrounds have their own native tongues but they all use design as a second language.

*Language is a city to the building of which*
*every human being brought a stone.*

MARK TWAIN

Design as a language of visual and material culture is also subject to the changes that collectively transpire within a culture. Like any language, design is an evolving social entity, and as societal realities intermittently alter our lifestyle they impact our values and consequently our aesthetics. Changes in the environment, economics, technologies, politics, and the sciences, for example, are always accompanied by contextual transformations in thinking that invariably remodel the nature of design. Because the vocabulary of our visual language is restyled as it interacts with everything from urban planning to interactive websites, it affects aesthetic judgments and, in the spectrum of ceramics, reshapes the dynamics of working with clay. This duality strikes me as being extremely ironic—that on the one hand design influences culture while on the other culture influences design. Still, it explains why ceramics from, say, the 1920's and 1930's is so different from what is being made today.

With any language, communication is only a problem when people aren't open to new ways of seeing. The same is true with design. When the Eiffel Tower was erected for the 1889 International Exhibition, the aesthetic language of its design personally offended the majority of Parisians. They found it to be incomprehensible. Held captive by cherished traditions, they felt threatened and saw it as a great insult to their city. Today this immense design of ironwork by the river Seine is the revered symbol of Paris. Likewise, when California artist Peter Voulkos started distorting large clay plate forms in the 1960's by poking and tearing into their surfaces, a majority of people in the clay profession were shocked. Back then they scoffed

John Brickels, *Buick Barn*

at the work but now the ridicule has turned to admiration and the name Voulkos is legendary in the world of art. Over time changes occur, but if we too want to do amazing things and have an immediate impact on clay we'll need more than hopes and wishes. We'll need to become action-oriented and that means being visually conversant in the design vernacular of artmaking. Art is language and language is communication, yet communication doesn't always easily occur. Otherwise we'd all be Voulkoses. Thankfully, I don't want to be someone else . . . but I do want to be the best of me, and what better way to discover who we are and what we know, feel, and think than by creatively working our way to the completion of a work of art. That's communication with a thread of sustainability running through it.

*Good design, at least part of the time, includes the criterion of being direct in relation to the problem at hand—not obscure, trendy or stylish. A new language, visual or verbal, must be couched in a language that is already understood.*

IVAN CHERMAYEFF

These days there are many issues surrounding exchanges of information: some that affect the nature of our clay work, others the nature of humanity. Some are unavoidable, possibly because as Christopher Morley points out, "life is a foreign language" and "all men mispronounce it." Others are simply out of our control because not everyone is aware of the multi-layered connections existing between things. Many don't see that design is as important to the shape of clay as it is to that of a kitchen, a pen or a community for living—or that all designs are interconnected and interrelated through a universal language alive with human meaning.

At the same time it's important that we as ceramists use the universal language of design without ignoring the impact of our choices. It is ultimately up to each of us to define the standards of our own vocabulary and with integrity evaluate its long-term contributions. As artists we speak independently; as human beings we speak collectively. The fact that Michelangelo's overpowering sculpture of *David* is so astonishing and marks him as one of the preeminent artists of all time is due in no small way to the personal standards he set and maintained for himself. In addition, he spoke in concert with the purest of voices to the shared heart of our humanism. For us to ensure that our clay pieces manifest our standards we have to ask ourselves the obvious: What is authentic and true to me? And just as importantly, how do I communicate that authenticity?

With thoughtful answers to such important questions we can begin to formulate our own design vocabulary and initiate the creative process that allows us to reconnect with ourselves and communicate with others.

3

# Design as Spirit

*A design is a song of man's creative spirit sung in harmony*
*with the spirit of mankind.*

AUTHOR UNKNOWN

There are any number of invisible qualities of silent grace and settled powers that hold us close and make a difference in all that we
do. Yet at any and every moment of our existence there is one dynamic quality to our being that reveals the mysteries of our creative existence and that is the human spirit. Through its ever-un-
folding nature it touches the pulse of all that we do, including
the contours of our clay. Like many things we can't see it can be
complex to embrace, but nevertheless it's capable of transferring
enormous amounts of energy and purpose to our designs. Without an alliance with the human spirit, designs lack a meaningful

Margaret Boozer, *Red Dirt Rake Print #2*

presence, surviving as efforts of what we do and not as affirmations of our wholeness—of spirit.

Design as it is referenced in these pages refers to the overall direction and physical resolution of a work of clay. To be sure, design is the undaunted power behind great works in clay, but it only exists in service of the artist to release, organize, and express inner dimensions of being. By directing the continual flow of creative energies, the design component is a constant companion to the spiritual heritage of our individual authenticity. Together they can be extremely successful. Working in combination they can bring value, completion, and validation to works of clay—an unforced blossoming of work and self.

*There is a vitality, a life force, an energy,*

*a quickening, that is translated through you into action,*

*and because there is only one you in all time,*

*this expression is unique.*

MARTHA GRAHAM

Design as spirit derives information from heightened states of awareness, from that part of our being that's tuned in to a higher and more enlightened sense of self. This higher, wiser self is the self that knows better. It is the self that is integrated with the fullness of our being. It's been called *conscience*, *the gut*, *the Divine mind*, *the God within us*. Whatever its name, it's the truth of our knowing. It knows and is known intuitively. It helps us to love in the midst of anger. It helps us to remain self-assured in the face of criticism and embrace confidence when surrounded by uncertainty. It helps us find beauty where there is unattractiveness and it gives us permission to be at peace. It grants us the freedom to say "yes" or "no." It gives insight into creative alternatives. And if that weren't enough, it puts trust into action.

As an intuitive quest for visual solutions, design is what ultimately brings personal resolution to artmaking. Its final outcomes, however, can never be predetermined. In other words, it proceeds without guarantees. As a creating process that continuously confronts choices it has no time line. How and when it ends is often another one of those unanswerable questions.

The same can hold true for knowing yourself. Along the way opportunities for learning arise and can range from a slight tingling of self-reflection to sensory flashes of aspirations. Just by living through a *design quest*—a period of extreme creative flexibility—we can go from feeling hopeless to feeling validated, if not outwardly at the very least inwardly. In many instances, living and designing cannot be pre-planned or blueprinted. So much of what is life and what is design unfolds from moment to moment and not all options can be foreseen in advance. For the ceramist, this power to choose between options is a treasured responsibility and as such it is a gift of freedom.

*Freedom is the open window*
*through which pours the sunlight*
*of the human spirit and human dignity.*

HERBERT CLARK HOOVER

All unconventional choices call forth freedoms. I am not suggesting, by emphasizing the role of free will in the designing process, that it is the only path to product. Still, I believe some of the most serious and daring design choices we make are rooted in the diverse freedoms thriving in our spirits. They expressively expand our

Jim Kraft, *Log Jam #3*

dreams and our internal desires to accomplish them. They qualify our intentions and, partnered with our experience, give rise (as acts of external completion) to a state of internal confirmation. Designing, like working with clay, always has its own inner rewards.

Designing is also a process of give and take. As it puts into operation forces of choice there are experiences, some positive and loving and others agonizing, which simultaneously give rise to both patience and doubt. Not all design decisions come together smoothly and work according to our wishes. Sometimes all we are left to do is remain still and avoid rushing blindly forward until fresh options present themselves out of the shards of the past. Being always vigilant to the constancy of self in the midst of life's ongoing changes is necessary. With faith and trust in the center of our own knowing we're able look deeper into ourselves for meaningful openings to those sought-after answers.

*Creativity is that marvelous capacity to*
*grasp mutually distinct realities and draw a*
*spark from their juxtaposition.*

MAX ERNST

Acknowledged consciously or not, design is a spiritual contract. Refusing to view it as such is an emotional dodge—one that could leave you settling for less than you deserve. If you are at all like me, you too have had a taste of tradition that told us what good design was, and yet nowhere was the human spirit even occasionally mentioned as being a part of the mix. On how many occasions have we stubbornly stood by and continued to work on a clay piece that was unnervingly being dragged down by weak design. Embarrassing— yes, but necessary—no.

The problem is that design (good, honest, authentic design) is not just a response to external circumstances and constraints. In many ways it is everything but external. Rather, it is more like a relationship shared between good friends. Although friendships may, and often do, respond to external situations, their ultimate development is dependent upon indispensable internal connections that are recognized and celebrated by each individual. In friendships the connections are internal yet their evolutionary growth processes occur in accordance with life experiences. This is precisely the same situation with design. Designing is a process that creatively occurs within us and as such is a reflection of our life experiences.

Like friendships, designs are very powerful and once they're created they have a spirit all their own. Both represent an intimate convergence and reflect the spiritual development of the individual with regard to awareness, commitment, and experience. They require that all of our perceptions and feelings be alive within us and that we ourselves be alive in the present.

*The ones who count are those persons*
*who—though they may be of little renown—*
*respond to and are responsible for*
*the continuation of the living spirit.*

MARTIN BUBER

All designs, like all individuals, are unique. The clay works that we create are one-of-a-kind for an infinite number of reasons, yet the essence of each work's nativity is the same: it is infused with the transparent energy of our design spirit, our spirit of what design is.

Creative pathways traverse the territory of spirit, which is why the visual life and vitality of any work of art is directly dependent upon the design spirit of the artist. The spirit of design is mysterious and more often than not rationally indescribable. But if its invisible tenets are lacking or out of balance the work is, for all intents and purposes, void of artistic consequence and aesthetically desiccated. Without a healthy infusion of spiritual subjectivity, the soulful reverence of a face-to-face exchange between the functioning forces of spirit and the genesis of design is conspicuously absent, sabotaging the success of the artmaking process.

*What is real is not the external form,*
*but the essence of things.*

CONSTANTIN BRANCUSI

Aesthetic desiccation is a lot like physical dehydration. As humans we are mostly composed of water (with 75% in the body and 85% in the brain). Water regulates all the functions of our body; without it the physiological components of our bodies are useless—with it they are activated. Clay as material relies upon water for its workability just as our bodies do, but clay as form relies upon the internal state of our aesthetic judgments for the essential well-being of its visual life.

On a medical or scientific level there is a direct correlation between a lack of water and illness. Water is the source of human life. With water, toxin buildups are flushed away and cures can occur naturally at a much faster rate than with medication. In the same way that we might not have focused on water as important for the vitality of our own health, we may also have failed to understand the importance of sensory awareness to the life of our ceramic works.

Craig Underhill, *Sun on Horizon*

Aesthetic desiccation renders clay work arid and lifeless. Just as we need to be responsible caregivers to our bodies we have a similar responsibility as form-givers to our clay to understand, recognize, and develop visual solutions that do not suffer from a kind of design drought.

> *When you reach the end of what you should know,*
> *you will be at the beginning of what you should sense.*
>
> KAHLIL GIBRAN

Another important concept is that design is spirit, not matter. Ultimately it is our spirit, not our hands, that gives guidance and shape to physical materials. Through a number of universal pathways called *design elements* and *design principles*, the creative force of spirit establishes the natural directions of our clay work. Together these two design entities create an opportunity, an opening, for our expressive self to enter the medium of clay and in a purposeful way they illuminate our work with the governing presence of our own spiritual gifts. Through the transforming forces of design we willfully reside in our clay. Just as we are alive in our natural spirit, our spirits are alive and immortalized in clay.

For the ceramist there are many spiritual pathways that give guidance to the creative process. The intangible enchantments of spirit can take many forms and are most significant when they promote truth, not lies; giving, not taking; or my heartfelt favorite, unconditional love, not self-indulgence. As you may begin to see, so much of what we do with clay and with our life moves first through spirit. For instance, before my wife and I were physically joined in marriage we had become one in spirit. The spiritual dimensions of unconditional love brought new meaning to our togetherness—one that has remained a lasting cause for celebration. Our relationship has been, thenceforth, memorialized in spirit even before being commemorated in marriage, so that to this day whenever we're separated physically we remain deeply connected spiritually. In a similar fashion, before our clay can be an object or vessel of our own truth and love it has to first originate as a vision of spirit. Our spirit as a creative reflection of our being is what gives value to all of our relationships, all of our clay forms, and just about everything else in life that we approach creatively. What we do in art and in life is therefore terribly important, for if what we do is not infused with spirit it lacks the capacity to transform the inner lives of others—as well as our own.

*Any relations in a social order will endure,*
*if there is infused into them some of that spirit*
*of human sympathy*
*which qualifies life for immortality.*

GEORGE WILLIAM RUSSELL

Design as spirit is an evolving gift of privilege on the lifeline of artistic awareness. Any awakening of inner resources is an epochal event in that it advances a vision of new opportunities for creating with greater freedom and fewer limitations. By living in the full consciousness of our spirit we have great leadership advantages and by extending that consciousness into our design activities we invite others to move forward in their journeys, encouraged by our initiatives.

Clay objects that have an authentic origin possess an aura, whether physical or not, that is capable of touching places of shared understanding in others. In certain cases the energy sent forth can be powerful enough to penetrate the spirit. Such connections can alter the actions of others in both physical and karmic ways which is why our capacity to relate to ceramic forms, whether viewing them or creating them, is often dependent upon the ability of the artist's spirit to live within the work and share itself with the open-minded spirit of others. This also explains how one work of clay can arouse so many warm and keyed-up sensations while another can leave us cold and indifferent.

As a ceramic artist and teacher of ceramics, my experience and concerns have frequently taken me in search of the more virtuous sources of creative artmaking. These are places that, if you're seeking to behold the mysterious workings of life itself, reveal certain universal truths that may previously have gone un-noticed and come to life within the workings of consciousness. As you can tell from the title of this book and the words on these pages, I have come to realize that the practice of design enlivened by spirit provides the major resources needed for outfitting our creative efforts, so that whenever we enter into that unmapped terrain of Mother Earth (i.e. clay) we do so with more than a set of clay tools.

Not surprisingly, I have also come to believe that our design spirit is acutely aware of the life around us. If it weren't it couldn't impress itself upon the situation at hand and initiate the needed res-olutions. After all, isn't this the primary function of the designer—to bring creative resolution to the task at hand? I would also like to add that the spirit finds its most visionary expressions through those who are candidly receptive to its nature and who recognize its po-tential to encompass all that is life. Design as a spiritual experience between our clay and ourselves reflects our ability to hook up with the spiritual flow of life and apply it to the shaping of our clay in a number of creative ways.

*The key to growth is the introduction of higher*
*dimensions of consciousness into our awareness.*

LAO TZU


Design is more than a field of study, an industry, or even a philosophy. Like love it has its definitions, but it also just happens. It happens like a sudden insight that uncovers a needed solution to a problem, as if there were a spontaneous realignment of magical forces that show the way forward to a meaningful completion. It also happens when there is a willful interest as designs and love both vibrate with the poetic fullness of our idealism, for each is an ideal that gives greater meaning to human life. We know this reality, sadly enough, to the degree that we have been haunted by its absence. There is emptiness in clay work that is devoid of design just as there is meaninglessness in life devoid of love. The dilemma here is that we may know what we want or need without knowing how to achieve it.

What often keeps us from claiming the truth of our desires is hidden in our misunderstanding of what they are. By focusing the greater part of our energy on externally motivated notions of success and none on the spirit of loving or the spirit of designing we fail to affirm the priority of our authentic self, thereby becoming unable to actualize the inner resources of spiritual wisdom.

Our spirit is the energy of our authentic self. Spirit energy is creative energy. Physically imperceptible, this energy resides deep within us and is often experienced as a wellspring of feelings. Feelings of spirit are liberating and because they don't contradict who we are they become spontaneously mobilized and supportive of our actions, making them rich and meaningful to our lives—especially in terms of what we do with our lives.

If we overvalue external things we undervalue our spirit. The value and meaning of life isn't found in things. Real meaning is found

Monique Muylaert, *Ruimte III*

within us and requires an internal way of seeing that values the intuitive gifts of our spirit. Love that is experienced internally and extended outward gives meaning to life. As an expression of self in the physical world, designs have meaning when they become effective instruments of spirit. A design born of spirit is like a stone thrown into a pond: it sends forth ripples of expanding circles. Each circle encompasses not only the spirit of self but continues to expand and evolve outward into ever greater circles of influence.

That's what design is: an expanding extension of change from the inside out, a releasing of spirit, a new orientation of self and an aliveness to creative work.

*A work of art is a world in itself, reflecting*
*senses and emotions of the artist's world.*

HANS HOFMANN

Our spirit is a natural gift but our designs are a spiritual achievement. The human spirit does not need to be created, only validated. Through spirit the design process is endowed with personal relevance. It brings a personal truth and character to clay that technique alone is incapable of providing. So stop calling your clay work *ceramics* or *pottery* and start calling it *art*. Acknowledge the creative viability of spirit that allows it to inspire the artist within and lead the design process forward. Then watch in wonder. One is often surprised at the number of veracious sparks of inspiration that unexpectedly—and I might add miraculously—appear when the spirit is reinforced with trust. The connections between spirit and design are so primal that they almost go unnoticed, but whenever we seek to bring our work to some unspoken sense of completion their interrelationship fortuitously reappears.

Timothy Ludwig, *Lidded Jar with Crown Imperial*

Spirit and design are co-creative forces. Together they become the heart of artmaking, not alternative options. This transformational crossover was summed up perfectly by two of my students. First when Kathy Schmelzer, with a sudden burst of excitement as if just discovering an enchanting secret, proclaimed, "Ceramics isn't clay: its spirit!" And again during a shared conversation on the aesthetics of throwing, only this time in a tone of quiet reflection when Stuart Shulman poignantly said, "A pot made without soul is just some clay around a hole."

# PART II

# Cultivating Your Design Aesthetic

*The object isn't to make art, it's to be in the
wonderful state which makes art inevitable.*

ROBERT HENRI

# Self-understanding:
# the Origins of Design

Through our thoughts, beliefs, and actions we create our own reality. By understanding this powerful truth we're in a better position to sidestep creative blocks and focus our will towards manifesting the designs that we visualize.

For example, there comes a time in our artistic life when technical issues take a back seat to those of expression. When that happens the 80/20 rule quietly comes into play where a large percentage of effect results from a small percentage of effort and the greater part of a design's development is derived from a self-liberated understanding of who we are—that small but very dynamic center of acknowledged authenticity. Through a knowledge of self we empower our spirit and infuse our life with a greater truth of being. As this user-friendly change takes place our departure to higher levels of awareness gradually converts mundane approaches to living into creative ones—initiating the origins of a reality where our designs truly exist as extraordinary extensions of ourselves.

If you're seeking to cultivate your personal clay aesthetic you have to consciously make the commitment to define and create your reality. Creative people generally accept the idea that their life is their creation and that if they are not acting from their own uniqueness they are simply doing what everyone else is doing and creating what everyone else is creating. The bottom line here is to respect your sense of self because if you don't your aesthetic identity will be tiresome even to yourself and your designs will be anything but original.

Respecting yourself is seeing who you are with a natural sense of self-assurance. Why is this important? Because being creative entails an internal approval of self. This inner self, overflowing with creative possibilities that others can't imagine, is one's real artistic center. The feelings, courage, and spiritual subtleties from which our designs grow are housed here. At times it's hard to comprehend, but once you understand this it will give you a great deal of personal command.

*Knowing others is intelligence;*
*knowing yourself is true wisdom.*
*Mastering others is strength;*
*mastering yourself is true power.*

LAO TZU

Join me now in looking at the various ways we can bring a more evolved self into the design process. I think you'll find the next five chapters surprisingly useful.

# 4

# The Creative Spirit

*First, one seeks to become an artist by training the hand. Then one finds it is the eye that needs improving. Later one learns it is the mind that wants developing, only to find that the ultimate quest of the artist is in the spirit.*

LARRY BRULLO

Physical relationship or spiritual partnership? How we view our connection to clay is a powerfully creative tool, yet we seldom give it consideration.

In our haste to become technically competent with our medium we often fail to grasp our dependence on the non-technical forces of art making. Complacency in such matters is all too tempting, especially if the creative flow isn't feeling obstructed. Still, it's seldom too late to transfuse our work with the energy of our humanness as well as our artistic skills—if inner resources are utilized. Let's face it, if we're not transferring those same expressions of spirit that shape our life to the shaping of our clay, we're not meeting our creative skills within the intimacy of a partnership.

The same is true for all artists, not just ceramists. Whenever the realization is made that self-expression is just that—an expression of self—they become less concerned with the final impact of their work and more actively involved in paying homage to who they are and what they can do creatively. We've always been attentive to how others perceive our work, but whenever we enter into new involvements with ourselves we become increasingly aware of how the work affects us personally. Essentially what happens is that we seek a more enthusiastic partnership between our self and our work. As a willingness to commit creative energies to working with clay increases, our awareness progresses beyond our initial bonding with tactile sensations and skill achievements until we are in full partnership with clay in a spiritual context. Through a spiritual give-and-take everything takes on new meaning and the importance of design suddenly catches us by surprise. Design in union with a creative spirit is recognized straight away as a winning combination for finding the completion we long for, both physically and spiritually.

> *Great dancers are not great because of their technique;*
> *they are great because of their passion.*

MARTHA GRAHAM

However difficult it is to envision a creative spirit it does exist as we are all inherently creative. But giving it a lean, precise definition is not always easy, partly because it's tricky to recognize it. When Confucius said, "Everything has its beauty but not everyone sees it," he too was familiar with the hardships of comprehension. As strange as it may seem, there are also those who don't yet know they have a spirit. Not only are they a long way from this discovery, they are even further removed from spanning the creative gap between the physical and the spiritual. In short, they have yet to distance themselves from ego domination and its resistance to genuine insight.

The ego is that self-centered part of our belief system that detours our judgment to the extent that it works against us. Ego does not endorse creativity. It thwarts it. It diminishes it and undermines our self-worth in the process. When I started out in ceramics I assumed that an "artistic ego" was a valuable and necessary asset. Consequently I spent an inordinate amount of time attracting exhibitions and observers. During those early years of excessive resume building and self-marketing I was separated from the true center of my creative energies. My ego had the upper hand and my creative spirit was eclipsed, its wisdom hidden.

Our wisdom is most expansive when it permits us to understand things as they really are. The ego, however, is not in favor of us having the knowledge and wisdom of understanding. It prefers that we live within the insecurity of fear and ignorance. Taken seriously, the creative spirit can direct our artistic life far better than the ego can. Like the ego, it too is physically unperceivable, but the spirit is a far more constructive force. As the true source of our creative identity it gives us the courage to look at our creative inheritance with wider expectations and greater purpose of use.

*Most powerful is he who has himself*
*in his own power.*

SENECA

Ken Eastman, *Nova*

The real value in living and working with clay is not just creating things that make us happy but to create things that illuminate our spirit. We can be open to life and alive in our work with clay and still live with an ongoing feeling that something is missing, where we are left somehow unfulfilled or lost at day's end.

True happiness and contentment is not achieved by how productive or technically proficient we are with clay, but rather by how good we feel about who and how we are with the clay. It involves knowing that we haven't compromised any aspect, any blessing of self in being who we are at every moment of the experience.

As the field of ceramics reaches for new horizons, ceramists are at the first light of a new era. Many are going beyond their physical relationship with clay and their knowing of self through bodily skills, entering a more expansive awareness of who they are, why they are here, and how they express themselves. This is a unique time in the history of ceramics, a time for claiming freedom and responsibility in a field that has traditionally been constrained and self-denying. It's a time for honoring the unification of design with personal spirit in an occupation that has been all too frequently aesthetically complacent and skill-structured. In short, this is a time unlike any other when we can claim the authenticity of our spirit, deepen our understanding of design's value, and walk away with a new medley of transcendent choices with which to gift ceramic forms.

"Most of the shadows of this life", wrote Ralph Waldo Emerson, "are caused by our standing in our own sunshine." A fulfilling relationship with clay goes beyond shadows and paradigms of the past. It even outdoes the pride of mastering techniques in handbuilding, throwing, and glazing and enters a more expansive realm energetically aligned with spiritual union and partnership. A truly fulfilling encounter with clay involves living in harmony with our authenticity and creating works whose design contributes in every way possible to the spirit of that authenticity while bringing forth the fullness of our human potential, our highest good.

*The only things in my life that compatibly exist*
*with this grand universe are*
*the creative works of the human spirit.*

ANSEL ADAMS

The act of making art, of making the unseen visible, is always a spiritual adventure. In the same way that the authenticity of our human spirit is not a physical substance neither is it sentimental, as sentimentality almost always yields to self-indulgence. As a matter of self-truth, spirit is a transcending force of creative energy that instills our life and artmaking with meaning. It is a venturesome source of courage, bravely sketching out designs for the tapestry of our life as well as the art that extends from it. Aside from being daring pathfinders, our creative spirits become great champions of our artistic identity. Once the very nature of our spiritual heritage is realized everything within us changes. Not only does our world become bigger, it becomes easier. Our ability to creatively transform thought and feeling into physical form is no longer the struggle it once might have been. Identity in partnership with spirit brings a new balance to life that allows creative energies to resonate with greater freshness and freedom. This inner balance is a very reassuring force. By providing a sense of inner calm and confidence it strengthens the uniqueness of our being and allows for more frequent opportunities to tap into deeper energies of self as well as those energies in the world around us that we may never have known we were part of. This occurs not only because life energies attract similar life energies, but simply because energy generates energy.

*The aim of art is to represent*
*not the outward appearance of*
*things, but their inward significance.*

ARISTOTLE

Chris Staley, *Alchemy Still Life*

Our willingness to recognize the spiritual dimension of our identity and to allow our designs to be an acknowledgement of it is the most important gift we can give ourselves. By embracing the domain of identity as a spiritual self we unite the core of our creative center with the creative center of humanity. In the spiritual universe of humanity there is a shared understanding between individual and collective identities that reveals our interconnectedness to all that is created.

As the designers of our clay work we can make a creative difference by getting to the source of our authenticity and bringing forth the best that is within us. Without a connection to our spirit it is almost impossible to be artistically authentic. As our capacity to create within a spiritual context expands, the center of our creative self becomes an unlimited resource. From an artist's perspective this spiritual center is the indispensable essence of the creative self and as the channel through which genuine art streams it exists in a state of continuous evolution. Comprehending the complexity of its evolvement is pivotal to how we shape clay and experience life.

*The object of art is to give life a shape.*

WILLIAM SHAKESPEARE

Design is the fourth dimension in ceramic art. It is very literal and very real. In subtle yet powerful ways its energy has a strong influence on the total functioning of every thing made in clay. When taken to heart, the enormous force of this aesthetic component is highly personal and therefore decidedly spiritual.

Because an understanding of design is something that is caught more than taught it becomes necessary to stay connected, at almost any cost, to the basic state of our being and to the insights this so uniquely provides. This connection with self is the basis of our spirituality. It is also what animates our clay. By embracing the design and fabrication of work with spirit we begin to create in ways that are simple and natural in their moment-to-moment evolvement. In doing so our spirit becomes more than a window through which we see: it becomes a doorway through which we pass. As a means of passage it allows us to impart (and extract) meaning throughout a journey that is very much our own. Approached in this way there is no separation between being and doing. The two are joined together and take on a sacred dimension.

*In the creative act, the artist goes from intention to realization through a chain of totally subjective reactions.*

MARCEL DUCHAMP

Whenever there is a design problem our spirit plays a creative role in its solution. In fact I doubt if there is any problem it cannot resolve. The key to understanding this is in realizing that the human spirit is not detached from our creative life but is an integral part of it. Its untold influence is intimately woven into the basic fabric of our being. In clarifying our vision, our spirit lights the way for us to meet our creativity and greet our originality at the crossroads of self-acceptance and self-awareness. It is precisely at this juncture that we can pinpoint the purpose of our being and with an open heart and mind begin from who and where we are now.

Not only do our clay works honor the truth and depth of this part of our being, they also nourish it by expanding our gratification. The most important component in this generative circle of fulfillment is the artist himself. If he is at all spiritual he lives within the strength and understanding of his inner nature. He has knowledge of who he is. And of equal importance, he is someone who is genuinely interested in putting that knowledge into action.

Knowing what we are is also important. If this weren't true we wouldn't be able to commit ourselves to those activities needed to achieve specific outcomes. With the focused awareness of knowing that we are ceramists who create in clay, our life has a specific direction that is propelled by spiritual energy. When lacking direction, life lacks personal energy and the gifts of the universe no longer avail themselves to us. It is through this recognition of self that our design skills are liberated and gain a directional focus. Put simply, the basis of our successes in clay come from who we are as well as what we do. For what we do is an articulation of who we are and by doing something that we have a gift for doing we also become what we are—an expressive extension of our creative spirit.

*Life is too complicated and there is too much*
*at stake to even think about trying to handle it*
*all without the guidance of the spirit.*

C. SMITH SUMNER

Any disconnect between our clay work and the authenticity of our life affects the success and well-being of each. If we are going to extend our love, time, and energy to working with clay we also have to do it with ourselves. Everything we can learn about our creative selves provides us with a knowingness, a new mindset that we can take back to the studio. This knowledge is a part of our spirituality and an important part of our learning how to empower clay. It is the first step towards taking direct responsibility for the quality of our designs. The final step is being responsible for what we do without exceptions or excuses.

*If it is to be, it is up to me!*

(10 IMPORTANT TWO-LETTER WORDS)
AUTHOR UNKNOWN

One critical responsibility of the designer is to stay alert and alive in the here and now. Design, like love, can only be fully experienced in the present. If we live outside of the present moment we are left unfulfilled. It's true that there's value to the artist in traditions just as there is in techniques, but these alone do not determine the value of the final outcome of what we create. For example, there is no greatness in mastering a technique from the past unless it allows us to escape its domination. Through playful living and spontaneous creation in the moment, designs have the freedom to develop in a way that makes them real. Our deepest insights are both felt and conveyed in the present. The most inspiring design decisions seldom come off a blueprint or out of a sketch book, they're expressed through human emotions as an aesthetic feeling fully engaged with a creative spirit in touch with the present. This experience of living and creating in the moment is a natural experience of fulfillment—an encounter with our deepest self which is where the joy of a creative life is really found. You may never be able to explain it but your clay will reflect it, for only in the present (during the brief workable life of clay) can the wholeness of a ceramic design conceive itself.

Elizabeth MacDonald, *Untitled*

*The miracle, or power, that elevates the few*
*is to be found in the industry, application,*
*and perseverance under the*
*promptings of a brave, determined spirit.*

MARK TWAIN

We are both physical and non-physical beings. Our physical body exists within the limitations of a material reality but our non-physical self—our spiritual self—is capable of experiencing limitless dimensions of consciousness. Our spiritual reality with its universal connections is our highest self. Our spirit, the essence of who we are, is the co-creator of our life. To recognize its unseen energy in everything we do is to understand the highest source of our creative powers. To respect the preciousness of our connection to this energy is the key to finding our happiness and peace in life. As an example, my wife and I are physical beings yet what exists between us in a non-physical context is so all-encompassing that it impacts every part of our existence in seemingly magical ways. Our physical nature, like many other physical circumstances, is necessary to the dynamics of our lives, but the miracle that I'll call the energy that is *us* is non-physical: it is spiritual. It has infused our relationship with an energy teeming with resolute faith, unconditional love, excitement, and celebration.

The spiritual nature of any relationship transcends physical limitations and because we are all spiritual beings we are subject to its implications. While there are those who don't yet know they have a spirit it does exists and it exists as one of our greatest assets. Without taking this sense of being into account, much in life remains veiled. Imagine how much loneliness and individual suffering is attributable to unrealized dreams or a life unlived. Awareness of one's spirit can affect the wholeness of every life situation.

*Life is finding yourself. It is a spirit of development.*

ROBERT HENRI

There is always a perceivable presence of spirit in our lives just as there is in our designs. It can affect our posture as much it does the shape and structure of our clay. Yet most of what accounts for its life-enhancing presence is invisible. Imagine for a moment that you just met me in person. You could observe any number of physical traits unique to me and still have little insight into who I am or why and how I do what I do. So much of what makes up the secret of who we are is imperceptible. Our intentions, attitudes, and a whole palette of thoughts, emotions, and feelings exist as part of our spiritual makeup. The value that I personally place on integrity, love, and family might easily go unseen in the physical world, yet they are three core values of my identity. As such they play a powerful role in my sense of self and lend strength to my spirit.

*And now here is my secret, a very simple secret;*
*it is only with the heart that one sees rightly, what is*
*essential is invisible to the eye.*

ANTOINE DE SAINT-EXUPERY

The spirit is the starting point for much of what enlivens our lives today—just as it is with our clay. It is a channel for finding the truth about ourselves and a conduit for our courage as we take risks to be more creative. Our creative spirit can also be our strength, our resolve for squeezing out the best of our talents. We have an inner capacity for creative genius that only our spirit knows how to coax out. By allowing the spirit to reveal the originality of self, talent and

Steven Hill, *Pitcher*

truth unite to become their own creative agency and together they bring a refinement to artistic form.

*Creativity is the voice of the spirit.*
*One's art should be the extension of oneself.*

MARITZA BURGOS

Every design experience is not just a new journey. It is an expedition into the living core of our emotional existence. For the ceramist it's a shaping of self as much as it is of clay which is a truth I learned as an art student. My first ceramics class, I thought, would revolve around my giving shape to clay. I had no idea, and I mean *no* idea, that the clay would end up reshaping my entire life. Even today I still marvel at how it happened and how I was touched by a medium that I thought could only receive touch.

As designers of our clay work we are taken to places where we may never have gone before. In the drama of shaping sculptural form from raw clay new realities of our inner world are revealed. Our perceptions become extended in all directions and perhaps for the first time, as happened with me, we go beyond current states of consciousness where we are secure in our rational views of self and object manipulation and become completely transformed. Places where a self once separate from experience now becomes the ex- perience, where self-awareness expands into collective awareness. In essence, where the self is no longer separate from the activity of creating. With this feeling of oneness, in artmaking as with all of living, we are able to function much more successfully because the barriers to our selfless use of energies, both our own and those in the world around us, are lowered. Once we transcend the need to experience everything from the comfortable confines of a self-centered space a whole new continuum of opportunities becomes available to us.

*You have to take it as it happens, but you should try to make it happen the way you want to take it.*

GERMAN PROVERB

In many ways our consciousness is the essence of who we are. With expansion of consciousness comes the liberation of self many of us have been seeking. As ceramists we also need to be impartial observers when we journey into the realm of the human psyche and explore the spiritual challenges of being creative. By maintaining a degree of detachment we can more or less enjoy the trip without being vulnerable to every bump along the way. Traveling along the altered edge of consciousness we encounter places that have remained unvisited and unseen. To stay the course we must keep our center—that tranquil place deep within that observes our activities but is not of their doing—if we want to experience the enjoyment that comes from not taking ourselves too seriously. Without fanfare the creative life is an enlightening adventure where we naturally have the true freedom to be who we are. Not only does it peer into places we may have unconsciously distanced ourselves from but it also leads into new habitats of the imagination that sustain those universal desires pulsating within all of us.

Matt Wilt, *Server*

# 5

# Universal Connections

*When we try to pick out anything by itself, we find it hitched to everything else in the universe.*

JOHN MUIR

As members of the same species we all share essential life elements. We may have different skin colors, speak different languages, or reside in different regions but we all have one basic thing in common: our spirits. Every human being has a spirit. It is what unites us all, unlocking the doors to the mysteries of our humanness. The human spirit is a life force—an energy—that enables us to live meaningful lives. As both the transporter and receiver of creative energies, our spirit exists and has always existed as the communication vehicle for universal expression and understanding between all of mankind.

Through spirit we are connected to every other living being as well as to those who are no longer with us. Exactly one week ago I was in Paris visiting the Louvre's art collection and had a chance to once again experience the work of Leonardo da Vinci. I have absolutely no idea as to what the specifics of this man's day-to-day life might have been like in 1504, but I do get a feeling through the reflective contributions of his art for what he knew to be true and real. There is an enormous power to perceive and actualize things in life when you are deeply connected to the innermost spirit of who you are and I cannot help but feel that Leonardo embraced a truthful dialogue with his spirit that allowed him to supersede the mundane and establish a higher connection to his life and to his work. Similarly, there isn't much I know or remember about my grandmother other than that she had a loving spirit that continuously emanated goodwill. For me that was the beautiful essence of her reality and the source of my great love for her. To this day her positive focus lives on as a silent strength behind my spirit.

*Everything that lives, Lives not alone, nor for itself.*

WILLIAM BLAKE

To live a creative life and birth strong works in clay requires a keen appreciation for spiritual relevancy. It's fairly easy to converse with those in our own surroundings. We speak in a common voice and share common ideas and cultural values with our immediate neighbors, but if we also want to have a meaningful communication with those in a foreign land or from a distant past we do so through spirit. The human spirit speaks a universal language that is not only timeless, but a revitalizing voice of life itself.

The visual elements and principles that form the language of design are and always have been universally understood. Throughout time people have both consciously and unconsciously assimilated

Velimir Vukicevic, *White Pitcher*

the richness of this language's infinite contributions. Whenever and wherever these visual principles are given expression through the openheartedness of an awakened human spirit, the artmaking is potent and humanity advances.

*Science and art belong to the whole world, and before them vanish the barriers of nationality.*

GOETHE

The language of design and the human spirit are two universal entities. Whenever they come together there is no absence of artistry and our worth as ceramists and as human beings is given new life. The challenges of designing clay works that transcend the status quo are best met with a loving spirit open to new possibilities rather than the lingering habits of the familiar. I always tell my design students that any solution that appears too predictable should be avoided. By expanding our dreams and engaging our spirits, designing can take a more innovative direction with less restrictive options.

Learning about these universal connections is like discovering the cosmos itself where an integrated and ordered system exists as a harmonious whole. Learning about the influence of our spirit on the success of our designs is central to the liveliness of our work. Ceramists are searching and they want their work to be as effective as it can be. To that end compelling works of clay reside within an inspired spirit.

The impact of the spirit on human judgment and behavior is elusive, yet most of us accept the influence of its energy on our consciousness. As ceramists our work mirrors our consciousness. It exists as a reflection of our spirit. If one's spirit is hardened and perpetually void of joy or satisfaction, one's clay work will be an expression of such an unhappy state.

*I'm in tune with the right vibrations in the universe*
*when I'm in the process of working.*

LOUISE NEVELSON

We both give and receive energy vibrations and it is up to each
of us to choose the life we live and how it will resonate in our work
and in the world. The way we see our life is the way we see ourselves
and vice versa. Which is why a spirit that embodies unconditional
love views the world it inhabits as a wonderful and beautiful place
despite threatening or fragile conditions. By taking responsibility
for ourselves we transcend the circumstances of our life and choose
to either disengage from what is happening or accept its manifestations. Either way, we're only free when we choose.

Our spirits are so interconnected that we frequently fail to recognize the impact their vibrations have on one another. Minute by
minute our spirits affect the world as they emit a continuous surge
of intermingling energy. There are no boundaries in space or time
to which they adhere and the impact they have on life is universal.
The spirit of love is one such example; nowhere is its infinite power
absent and at no time is spirit not in attendance at love's initiation.
It's like a soothing extrasensory wind that continuously touches the
reverence of our humanity.

*Gravitation is not responsible for people falling in love.*

ALBERT EINSTEIN

Design is our awareness put into action. If we choose to put it
into motion and apply it appropriately the changes it brings to life

Meredith Knapp Brickell, *Double Catch*

can be both effective and dramatic. If not nothing happens and we go on reliving our comfortable past, thus turning our own history against ourselves.

Ceramic creations are a direct result of applied awareness. Using the universal language of design, the visual depth of our perceptions finds a new way of generating innovative shapes in clay in the interconnections between being and creating. Any such awareness is a fresh shift in self-perception. If we fail to honor the chronicle of our own narrative or fail to recognize the glorious dynamics of universal influences we run the risk of displacing a sustained connection to the wholeness of life—not to mention the possibilities for a more expressive existence.

> *The whole of the visible universe is only*
> *a storehouse of images and signs to which the*
> *imagination assigns a place and*
> *a relative value; it is a kind of nourishment that*
> *the imagination must digest and transform.*
>
> CHARLES BAUDELAIRE

Any separation from awareness is a separation from self and a detour to a dispirited outlook and an uncreative path. Our creative identity is self-awareness transformed into inspired self-determination. Identity is a way of processing our take on life and the alternatives it presents to us. How we choose to align ourselves with the spiritual and creative energies of the universe defines us. The more responsive we become to identifying the genuine sources of our identity the more caring and enlightened our reactions will be.

Making an identity shift within our being from artificial to natu-

John Herbon, *Untitled*

ral responses allows us to feel more present in our creative activities. We live and create the truth of who we are, both personally and professionally, whenever we share a vision of ourselves that makes universal connections. The deep meaning of our truth is made more vibrant and less limiting when we realize that we are at one with a larger truth. While it is important for you to know you-as-you it is equally important to know you-as-universe. Living with an awareness of our connectedness is like holding the keys to the realities that unclutter life and move it forward.

Each of us embodies the ability to distinguish between our personal truth and its manipulation. The former sanctifies everything it comes into contact with while the latter undermines it. One triumphs as the other languishes. To know our truth we have to look past external pressures, appearances, and expectations. We need to find independence, to look within and earn our own approval. Eventually the greater knowledge of who we are emerges and our truth is not only revealed but more importantly it is trusted. With trust in our selves we totally—and I mean totally—know how to be creative with clay as well as with living our life.

*Self-trust is the first secret of success.*

RALPH WALDO EMERSON

So much of what happens in our world, our lives, and our art-making is the result of universal forces. The unfolding of these naturally occurring phenomena fall under several generic headings such as *universal laws, laws of nature, collective consciousness, divine law, laws of humanity* or, as in the context of this text, *the elements and principles of design*.

*No only is the universe stranger than we imagine,*

*it is stranger than we can imagine.*

ARTHUR EDDINGTON

Both internally and externally we are a part of so much more than we sometimes realize. The sun rises and sets, the tides ebb and flow, we inhale, we exhale. Lines, shapes, and colors hold their same universal place in the visions of designers today as they did a thousand years ago, the bottom line being that universal factors work together to move life forward. Each of us through creative living continues the birthing of the future.

In the big picture we are all a part of life and by way of that single truth we are one with the universe. Through awareness of this oneness we are able to accept the connections of our physical, spiritual, and creative self with the forces at work, both in the universe and within us.

*We are the leaves of one branch, the drops of one sea,*

*the flowers of one garden.*

JEAN BAPTISTE HENRY LACORDAIRE

Who we are is an infinite self: a shared entity whose essence is found in everyone and in all of humanity. The human sensuality, compassion, wonderment, and imagination in my consciousness is in yours as well. The love that remakes me remakes you too. We all live along a continuum of collective energies and none of us can function or create in a state of isolation or separateness. Everything we make of our life and with our life is in ongoing union

Margaret Boozer, *Red Fracture / Fill*

with universal forces. This in itself is a universal principle that graces our lives.

We don't create these universal happenings—we coexist with them. Through the powers of our awareness we mindfully co-create in partnership with them and in so doing we lend a delivering hand with the birth of what is yet to come. Should we fail to understand the certainty of universal connections or violate them through a lack of awareness or respect, or even worse through intentional resistance, we endanger not only the creative potential for artistic achievement in our lives but also the welfare of our physical and spiritual lives.

From the standpoint of our own individual spirit, the value of living with an identity that has universal connections is that it constitutes an indispensable source of our humanness. Our living identification with others becomes the heartfelt source of our own goodness and from the astute guidance of this understanding we can move onward and live a loving and compassionate existence—a meaningful life.

> *When one has weighed the sun in the balance,*
> *and measured the steps of the moon,*
> *and mapped out the seven heavens star by star,*
> *there still remains oneself.*
> *Who can calculate the orbit of his own soul?*
>
> OSCAR WILDE

All things work together and our design aesthetic is equally responsive to the vast wholeness that is life. As we come to see the connections operating in the whole of evolution and find assurances through universal truths, the miracles that happen in life can also be made to happen in our work. Design is not a science or a pre-packaged set of formulas and recipes. In so many ways it is simply an art. As an art its subtle complexities and corresponding life effects can tie more restrictive knots around our behavior than it unties. Creative freedoms are often repressed by underlying states of anxiety or fear. Our personal history of negative experiences can attest to those painful times when we were off our game, in unfamiliar territory, or just unable to connect the dots with any creative enthusiasm. As designers we can meet such challenges to our artmaking by tapping into the collectively honored structures of design. Accessing and applying these universally and historically established fundamentals can help strengthen the weak points in our creative responses and further link our intuitive sensibilities to a universal supply of timeless affirmations.

Herman Muys, *Koning En Koningin*

6

# Love Consciousness

*In order to create there must be a dynamic force,*
*and what force is more potent than love?*

IGOR STRAVINSKY

Love is inseparable from creativity. Where there is one you find traces of the other. Both thrive in a constant state of change, continuously intermingling with one another in a never-ending quest for a new emergence of expression. As two co-creative forces they become the inspirational foundation for distinctive designs to originate from. Together they give creative leadership to the ceramist. So before you ask the question, What does love have to do with design? understand that love is more than romantic passion; it is an energy that permeates the environment of creative possibilities. As an ongoing primal force it gives our clay work added direction and to the degree that it is integrated into the design process it empowers our work with greater purpose.

Creativity is love living within us. Whenever love is present life is valued differently and becomes less of a problem in need of solutions. When it's not present isolation, conformity, and fatefulness drag on. Love dispels acidic forces that harm rather than enhance our spirit and creativity. It is in love's nature to release us from the pressures of uniformity and transcend worldly controls so that we are free to follow our own course of travel. A loving spirit reverses worldly resistances and transforms our egocentric identity to where our freedom is linked to the universal concerns of humanity. It refocuses our values, moral responses, and social priorities.

What makes love so indispensable is that it invariably alters our intimate sense of self and initiates us into our humanness. It all begins with the fact that love is a great and powerful force which is why it is impossible to talk about the creative gifts of the human spirit without also addressing the consequential role that love plays. It is important to note that love is not the absolute source of either our creativity or our spirit since both already exist as innate qualities within us. It does, however, impact their purpose and ultimately our behavior.

*We are shaped and fashioned by what we love.*

GOETHE

Our spirit can be as positive, pure, and illuminating as the luminous sun in a cloudless sky or as negative, dark, and foreboding as the shadowy clouds in a storm. One's spirit can be good or evil, cruel or kind, productive or unproductive. Creativity can also be a double-edged sword used either constructively or destructively. Tied all together, love, spirit, and creativity become the definitive expression of our most revered values.

Human history is full of destructive events initiated by intelligent individuals who were wholeheartedly creative. Nevertheless—and this is the essential issue—their spirits became tragic forces of darkness that generated horrendous suffering. With regard to life it is clear that something was spiritually wrong and seriously absent. Essentially their spirits were lacking the virtuous radiance of real love. By putting their depraved agendas ahead of everything else they invariably manifested not only a disregard for others but also a profound disrespect for their own humanity.

*Hell is truth seen too late . . .*

TRYON EDWARDS

Unloving forces of greed and power belittle the true meaning of life which is simply to give and receive love. When genuine love takes up residence within our spirit we naturally become more open to ourselves, to others, and to life. It is often said that fear is the flip side of love. As we all know, when fear is present there is a numbing of the senses and it becomes more difficult to embrace the dynamics of selfless love within us. In the presence of love, self-acceptance flourishes and the inner confidence needed to be outwardly giving in a creative way steps forward ready to lead the way.

*Design is not making beauty, beauty emerges from*
*selection, affinities, integration, love.*

LOUIS KAHN

Gail Piepenburg, *Reflection*

Each of us will continue to suffer feelings of loss as war is studied more than love. Why are there huge military establishments, academies and war colleges, but only an occasional course on love? Is it more important to protect homelands than heartlands? I hope it's not due to any illusion that war is infinitely easier to justify or summon up as a solution. Or could it simply be due to cultural conditioning that values enmity and self-importance over the intuitive truth of human knowledge? Still, the dysfunctional reality of finding it easier (or in some way more worthwhile) to be at war rather than in love will always leave me in a state of bewilderment.

*No problem can be solved from the same level*
*of consciousness that created it.*

ALBERT EINSTEIN

Certainly love is honored and desired in this world but not nearly enough. Still, love stops more wars and acts of cruelty than it starts. Perhaps we could do better at defending homelands through the cultivation and practice of love's teachings than with military lore. How can so many human beings live in self-deception hiding from love's power? Are there egos at play here that only look for battles and resistance-laden responses? How long can the self betray itself? All of these questions relating to an absence of love might leave one feeling hopeless except for the fact that love and self-expression are contained within one another.

*When love and skill work together, expect a masterpiece.*

JOHN RUSKIN

Many of our perceptions should be replaced with love if we are going to find peace in the outer world and within ourselves. Our egos and society at large often place more importance on the successes in life—on influence, recognition, financial security, and a host of other power-oriented adventures—than on love itself. External circumstances may affect our willingness to deny or receive love, but whatever attention we choose to give it is of our own choosing. Love originates from within us. At all times we are responsible for our thoughts and actions. Sometimes we are victims of outside influences, but we are often the victims of our own loveless ways.

*If I create from the heart,*
*nearly everything works;*
*and if from the head, almost nothing.*

MARC CHAGALL

Through love we experience the nobility of our spirit and the dignity of our existence where life is us and we are life. Within this union we are able to know the true center of our being and with this knowledge realize that it does not—and never did—lie outside us. The power of our creative potential is not externally dependent on someone else's input or approval. As artists our designs are external expressions of internal love.

*I think one's art goes as far and as deep*
*as one's love goes.*

ANDREW WYETH

Matt Long, *Belly Button Cups*

Design is love manifest in physical form. If we only search for inspiration outside ourselves we can end up empty-handed, for what we do is really who we are and who we are is what we do. The same is true for love. If its blessings are not found within ourselves first and accepted with faith, trust, and tenderness, how can they ever be recognized elsewhere? Not accepting that we are lovable distances us from our spirit and the center of our humanity. It prevents us from embracing others in spite of any imperfections they will, like each of us, inevitably have. Weaknesses prevail in all of us, but true love is not so conditional or judgmental as to find ourselves and others unworthy. True love always affirms our worthiness. It allows us to be open to ourselves and settled in our being, in the real essence of who we are. It also makes it possible for us to receive love and recognition from others. And most affirming of all, it gives strength and nourishment to the seeds of our creativity.

# 7

# Self-love—
# Establishing Your Center

*You, yourself, as much as anybody in the entire universe,*
*deserve your love and affection.*

BUDDHA

Some of life's universal directives aren't always understood until their explicit guidance is needed and fortuitously offered to us over a plate of spätzen noodles.

All of us have experienced romantic love and the joys that only lovers can share. Unfortunately not all loving relationships endure. And if they end in betrayal or rejection the termination induces all kinds of pain and suffering. Many, many years ago a relationship in which I was deeply involved came to such a dark end. The months following were filled with loneliness and self-blame. They were dysfunctional times, and I was in need of emotional healing.

At the same time, while struggling with my grief, there was a restaurant called the Old German that I frequently patronized for dinner. In the city of Ann Arbor the Old German was an institution; it had a long tradition of serving good food in a European-style setting. What appealed to me the most, beyond its charm, was its community table. This was a large table intimately situated near the back of the restaurant where they would seat customers who were dining alone. It was at this table in conversation with a stranger that I was told I could come to my own aid if I embraced myself in the same heartfelt ways I would a lover. That evening I quietly reclaimed my center. It was literally a life turning point. The memory of that night's lesson is still with me and I continue to experience uncompromising feelings of love and respect to the deepest reaches of my being. It was also at this time that the golden rule went platinum by becoming more inclusive: "Do unto yourself and others as you would have them do unto you".

*You will always have to live with yourself, and it is to your best interest to see that you have good company— a clean, pure, straight, honest, upright, generous, magnanimous companion.*

ORISON SWETT MARDEN

So what is self-love? And what does it have to do with design? The answer to this second question is nothing, unless you accept the complex fact that the self as designer is at the foundational center of the design process. The designer is not a spoke in the artistic wheel. The designer is the dynamic hub—the axis around which resourceful innovation revolves. As to what is self-love, for a start it's safe to say that it is the root source of all the love in our life. With it we attract and extend love; without it love is lost and never lived. Self-love is also intimately tied to everything we do. It is self-referential. Our creativity, our relationships, our dreams—all our encounters with life—are a manifestation of either loving or not loving ourselves.

Likewise, our designs are inseparable from the love, respect, and caring we have for ourselves. The way we choose to shape our clay is a reflection of how we see ourselves. After all these years as a studio art teacher I remain awestruck at how much of an individual's intrinsic character, behavior patterns, and personal standards are revealed through their work activities and their creations. Authentic clay designs are an intermingling of self with material, not the mere manipulation and joining of leather-hard slabs. Clay works become dramatic expressions of a person's life and reflect the state of the artist's feelings. Neither the material nor the process is objectified or void of human intimacy when it exhibits the reality of the artist's disposition and temperament, for what we regard as good design or sanction as art is inseparable from self-expression and self-love.

*People are afraid of themselves, nowadays.*
*They have forgotten the highest of all duties, the duty*
*that one owes to one's own self.*

OSCAR WILDE

The intimacy of love, especially self-love, is needed to both explore and express our deepest passions and everything else that captivates an artist's imagination. Self-love is dynamic in its gifts of courage. As it leads us to new levels of self-acceptance it liberates our spirit and gives us an empowered strength of daring to forcefully move forward in life and be creative in our artmaking even when we don't know where things are headed. A consequence of this level of stalwartness is that it allows us to proceed into the voids of unknowingness and uncertainty without hesitation and accept the challenge that unintended things happen. A courageous sense of steadfastness and self-trust is what gives our designs their vitality and allows us to make creative breakthroughs when other sources of inspiration are unconvincing.

Living with self-love is as important to the unfolding of our ceramic forms as it is to the unfolding of our lives. There are elements of risk in life and in art. Still, the experience of our inner love teaches us to trust our inspirations and never betray the truth of our identity. For every step we take toward loving ourselves the truth of who we are takes a step toward us.

> *Truth is the first thing to be sought for, and Beauty and Goodness will then be added unto you.*
>
> MAHATMA GANDHI

To be artists capable of expressing the truth of our ideals requires that we not only discover who we are but that we also become who we are—our authentic self. Along with this inner realization of enlightenment it is important that we also enlighten ourselves to the concept of self-love. By loving ourselves we actualize the truth of our inner identity and achieve a state of individuality called "self."

> *Love the one you're with . . .* (you)
>
> CROSBY, STILLS, NASH AND YOUNG

Shozo Michikawa, *Square Incense Burner, Kohiki*

Self-love is also a link to our authenticity, that point where inner meanings and purpose come together to manifest a true spirit of self. It is a spiritual state that is in total harmony with itself and the universe. Spiritually the center of love is everywhere. And we establish our center within this ubiquitous center by the love we create for our self. Once our loving center is self-assured the process of extending love forward never ends. It becomes perennial, as does our ability to be creative.

The love we have for self is our spirituality. Alive within us, it is (as spirit) an energy source, a power through which the force of our creative gifts can flow with positive support. When this relationship is in sync with itself it resonates with visions of clarity that release new opportunities for transformational creative achievement. Through self-love we are alive to our artistic selves and the potential of our creative talents as well as worldly riches and prosperity.

*There is no one alive who is youer than you.*

DR. SEUSS

Our design process is not only connected to our feelings of self, it is dependent upon them. Long before a design image is actualized and becomes a physical presence in the world it is a non-physical sensation. These internal sensations are intermeshed with our human spirit and are made accessible through loving feelings of self. A true love of self calls forth an unremitting assortment of personal "can-do" sensations that inspire our designs long before we ever realize their properties as a physical experience.

To further understand self-love it is helpful to know what it is not. In no way is it a shallow, superficial, or false impression of self, nor should it be associated with vanity or pride. It is self-centered but it is not egotistical: it is not the ego itself. As a true love of self it is a principled prerogative, but not self-righteous or narcissistic. As an intuitive response to self it cannot be perceived through the physical senses as it is not of the physical world. It resides within each of us as the ultimate source of purpose in life, yet from time to time it remains hidden from our acceptance. Having no price tag it cannot be held accountable to worldly things that do not reciprocate and give love back. Its true value and significance aren't found in worldly domains but within each of us. As the love we have for ourselves expands we find that there is a meaning to life in extending that love out into the world in every way possible. As ceramists we can express our love creatively by always thinking of what we give through our designs, not what we receive. By honoring the life we have been given with the loving care and respect we extend to ourselves we provide ourselves with the energy to share our love with others. Not only through our joy, kindness, and compassion, but also through our object-making. A lack of self-love would have the opposite effect on our behavior and find us expressing selfishness, greed, and suffering. Through an unloving corruption of spirit, feelings of anger and frustration would surface and our creative edge would vanish.

*I love people. I love my family, my children . . .*
*but inside myself is a place where I live all alone*
*and that's where you renew*
*your springs that never dry up.*

PEARL S. BUCK

So how do we find the love of self that we seek, need, and deserve? First we must realize that we already are love and that we are

Sam Chung, *Teapot*

one with all that is love. In the same way that we are one with life and all that is life we are love. We are not separate from the universal whole, we are a part of it. And the more we understand our place in the dynamics of this grand interconnectedness the closer we come to discovering the fundamental nature of our selves and the clarity of our being. From this place of spiritual discovery it is quite easy to value the eminence of self and feel nothing but love for all that we are and all that we do. We also have to unchain ourselves from past practices and routines and trust in the self-determination of our own loving spirit. To be free to create with autonomy in the future we have to leave the conformity of the past. By renouncing our old-time egocentric images of self-importance we clarify our visions of reality. With a more wakeful eye we're able to view the nature of things as they are and not just how they appear. Clear-sightedness comes with a maturing love of self. Knowing that, I suggest we celebrate it and let it be an instrument of our creativity.

Creative Aspects of Self-love:

- It's adventurous (welcomes innovative ways of seeing and experiencing)
- It's intuitive (responds to the authority of inner moods, feelings, and insights)
- It's goal-free (enjoys the exuberance of the doing over the focus of achieving)
- It's trusting (feels confident in the resolution of any difficulty)
- It's detached (it is in our world but not of it)
- It's generous (finds unbounded joy in sharing and forgiving)
- It's courageous (provides freedom to act without inhibition)
- It's accepting (supplies unhindered self-satisfaction)
- It's respectful (honors the life and splendor of all things)
- It's compassionate (generates an unreserved passion for caring)

- It's non-discriminatory (does not respond from arrogance or insecurity)
- It's loving (harmonizes with the love around us)
- It's freeing (invites an unrestricted response to every experience)
- It's truthful (displays an internal loyalty to self)
- It's mindful (presents a meaningful awareness of existence)

You have often heard it said that we cannot love others if we cannot love ourselves or that others will not love us if we don't love ourselves. Sounds like a trade transaction doesn't it? Well, if there were such an exchange it wouldn't be called love. For love, simply stated, is an acceptance of self and/or another person. And real love is an acceptance of self and others that is unconditional, meaning without any conditions whatsoever.

The love we have for our self is vital to the love we experience in our life. It literally shapes every aspect of it and, consequently, our designs. Without a genuine love and respect for ourselves we—as a frenzied array of unsatisfied needs and insatiable appetites—have nothing of importance to give to our creations. With a love of self the opposite is true. The more we come to accept ourselves the less we are weakened by the insecure energies of self-doubt and low self-esteem. As we become more secure within ourselves a greater current of loving energy flows through us and into our day-to-day living as well as our moment-to-moment creating.

We intensify this energy and increase our development through a recognition of self that identifies with everything that is positive, good, and truthful in life. What was once automated compulsive behavior filled with emotional demands and expectations now becomes a transcendence of peaceful clarity.

*A man who becomes conscious of the responsibility*
*he bears toward a human being who affectionately waits*
*for him, or to an unfinished work,*
*will never be able to throw away his life.*
*He knows the "why" for his existence,*
*and will be able to bear almost any "how."*

VICTOR FRANKL

Behavioral research studies show that how we feel about ourselves determines how we live and affects our creative thinking. If
those feeling aren't supportive, self-compassionate, and self-forgiv-
ing our potential for becoming creatively enlightened is severely
limited. By failing to appreciate our own knowingness we fall short
in recognizing the source of our unique talents and capabilities.
Without a healthy realization of self there is a cheerless lack of confidence which involuntarily translates into a dismal lack of self-esteem. Mahatma Gandhi once said, "Life is an aspiration. Its mission is
to strive after perfection, which is self-realization." If we lay claim to
the radiance of our self-esteem, any conflicting feelings of repressed
inadequacies or lifelessness that may have curbed the efficient use
of life energies is replaced with new visions of self that can create
extraordinary change.

We can change the self-negating demeanor that defeats our
sense of worthiness but we have to initiate the change. And we have
to do it with a vow of commitment. For better or worse we are already wed to ourselves for the remainder of our lives. Annulment
and divorce aren't options—a loving relationship is. A commitment
to unconditionally love and cherish who we are might be the most
far-reaching gift of love our life could ever receive. And what a gift:
to have our own center of meaning in life!

*Inside you there's an artist you don't know about.*
*He's not interested in how things*
*look different in moonlight.*

AUGUSTE RODIN

Love is our only means of transportation towards a new emergence of self. It is also our only passageway to a useful purpose in life. Through it we are able to embrace life and be caring of it and because loving initiates loving it is a constructive, not a destructive, phenomenon. For this influential force to bring inspired leadership to our life we cannot ignore, forsake, or forfeit caring for ourselves. In this sense our work as designers can't begin until the more heroic work of loving ourselves is well under way.

8

# Spiritual Principles—
# Intimate Guidance

*Whatever is at the center of our life will be the source of our security, guidance, wisdom and power.*

STEPHEN COVEY

Where a lot of artists are at right now is a place of personal discovery where they realize that having a spiritual component to their artmaking is every bit as important as having it in their lives. This is especially true with ceramists. While this emergence may be due in part to the primal nature of clay itself, I think it is mostly a reality shift of consciousness. Any alteration of consciousness, like any process of internal transformation that leads to a new state or quality of being, can be likened to an awakening. If such discoveries lead to a deeper dimension of self they are in essence spiritual and add new purpose to being alive.

As for what exactly constitutes spirituality it is never easy to say, but we do know that it endows everything from art to politics with humanness. We also know that it is a precondition to our becoming—to the finding of our own authentic path in life—because spirituality gives intimate meaning and guidance to life. It is the sum total of energy that exists within our heart, mind, and body. Without it we are unable to recognize a deeper sacredness in life, let alone understand the creative process. If we acknowledge the importance of our spirit and its reverence for that which is universally true, positive, and wise then the next question becomes: "How do we take it into the studio?"

*Remember, the entrance door*
*to the sanctuary is inside you.*

RUMI

Unlike the elements and principles of design which are easily used and experienced at a physical level, our spirit isn't as confined. It is much more expansive. Once we've connected with a deeper sense of inner awareness, our knowing and our doing are governed by a series of spiritual principles that affect every aspect of our lives. Like artmaking, the forces governing our emotions, relationships, careers, and health (to name a few) are spiritual. The power of this awareness alone can be transformational and is a good starting point for making useful connections between spiritual energy and creative energy. Artist Ben Nicholson said: "A civilization can be gauged by the degree of equality reached between man and woman." I think it can also be said that the range of equality exercised between revelations of spirit and imagination can perpetuate a unity of expression that reflects the essence of design itself.

*Spirit borrows from matter the perceptions*

*on which it feeds and restores them to*

*matter in the form of movements which it*

*has stamped with its own freedom.*

HENRI BERGSON

The four spiritual principles I've chosen to focus on are *flow, manifestation, abundance,* and *nonattachment.* For me as an artist and a human being who acknowledges his spirit, these are mainstay principles as each encompasses universal truths that are in harmony with the dynamics of creative activity. Once applied, their contributions to artmaking are immediate and fulfilling. Before we explore these principles I think it's best if we first lay some groundwork upon which to examine their relevance.

To begin with, the ethical and aesthetic standards that define our spirituality, our philosophy, our identity, and more importantly in terms of artmaking our behavior, are derived from our values. It all starts with our core values and each of us, whether we fully recognize them or not, has an underlying set of subjective values that contributes to the fiber of our beliefs, ideas, actions, etc. Our value systems are internally prioritized and intrinsically define what is worthwhile and desirable to us and what is not—regardless of any external verification or lack thereof.

*That which is most personal*

*is universal.*

AUTHOR UNKNOWN

Nina Hole, *Boat*

Anthony Caro, *Summit Games*

Values develop from experience. They are resistant to change but nevertheless remain flexible and evolve as we do. When I was young, *family* wasn't a predominant value but now (after helping to raise five children) it, along with *love* and *integrity*, is one of my three core values.

There is a seemingly infinite number of human values, but when values are equated with the character trait of being and/or doing good (values such as *compassion*, *kindness* or *empathy*) they are also referred to as virtues. While many virtues aren't universally accepted, researchers have bundled those that are into the six separate categories of *wisdom, humanity, justice, courage, temperance* and *transcendence*—to which I'd also add *creativity*.

Classifications are helpful ways to look at, compare, and understand information, but how it all plays out depends on where they inspire us to explore next without missing what's currently before us. For some time now the five values of *integrity, intuition, trust, truthfulness* and *mindfulness* have been especially relevant to artistic success. To gain a better understanding of the guidance they lend to being creative, let's have a closer look at them.

*The only things in my life that compatibly*
*exist with this grand universe are the*
*creative works of the human spirit.*

ANSEL ADAMS

**Integrity**—Integrity is fundamental to harmony in life and has primal correlations to creativity. I have found a great deal of personal happiness and peace by making it the keystone of my value system and by allowing its presence to be a part of everything I do. I have come to identify it with my life: it is embedded within my sense of self and flows through all of my activities. It also gives inner direction to my artmaking. The profound effect of acting with integrity is that our personal truth becomes our creative truth. Artists who use its guidance to navigate in creative realms are the ones who create works that come alive and remain so in the rest of us. When creative activity is carried out with integrity it increases our ability to transcend confusion. As in life, when something goes wrong with our artwork it can often be traced to an integrity issue. With integrity comes enlightened clarity and a realization that everything is suddenly possible.

**Intuition**—Intuition can be a very mysterious thing. Resistance to it is not uncommon, yet it remains the key to authentic expression. Many artists prefer to be logical or rational in the studio, yet they often can't explain why or how they created what they did. As a natural faculty of comprehension, intuition is knowledge gained through spirit. It is an instinctive knowing, a self-sufficient knowledge that possesses more wisdom than our conscious mind can explain. The strength of its guidance can transform our creative flow through gifts of unexpected insights and purpose. In being creative the artist departs from reason and confronts the unknown, not just as an intellectual but as a visionary traveler whose creative life is a reflection of a deeper connection between spiritual sensibilities and current circumstances.

**Trust**—Trust is a necessity for artmaking. Not only is it the pathway to creativity but it is also an illuminating pathway to all of life's opportunities. It is an internal knowing that carries both life and work forward. Often our ability to move forward in life is far more dependent on how we feel about ourselves and our abilities rather than on external factors. Self-trust, for example, is self-loving and not self-neglecting. Trust fused with the fullness of our potential gives life and imagination to expression. Self-trust can nurture that expression, allowing us to do our best, whereas self-doubt can promote a sense of unworthiness. With trust living is easy. Through trust we have the clarity of spirit and the strength of our center to act. Without it our creativity is held captive.

**Truthfulness**—Truthfulness and truth are not the same thing. Truth is objective and externally visible. Truthfulness is a personal truth; it is internal and may or may not relate to external circumstances. In a creative context, artwork may be seen as an objective truth derived from the truthfulness of a deeply subjective experience. The creative person knows what is real and does not "fake" the truth of who they are. To do so would be a rejection of self. Our internal truth, because it is our personal power, is the truthfulness of our spirit and gives us creative strength. As with integrity, truthfulness resides in the essence of things more than it does in appearances.

**Mindfulness**—Mindfulness is a sensitized observance of life. It is what connects us to the details of our existence in meaningful ways. As artists, the more we come to understand our personal lives the closer we come to liberating our creative spirit. Creativity is bound to life and all of its truths and circumstances. By being attentive—mindful—to our life we not only experience a more peaceful and inspirational coexistence with living but we cultivate our creative potential as well.

> *Keep tight hold on the present. Every condition, every*
> *moment even, is of infinite worth because it is the*
> *representative of all eternity.*

GOETHE

Lorna Meaden, *Watering Can*

Each of us is a part of the universe that created us and because of that reality-truth we are in an inseparable relationship with it. In spite of our sociocultural conditioning we are an integral part of the universe's natural order.

In the same way values and principles are an integral part of our lives. What separates a universal value from a universal principle is that such principles are timeless and do not change over time. A principle is a broad, basic, and undisputed truth upon which other essential truths rely. A universal spiritual principle is the essential functioning of natural phenomena through subjective standards of conduct. For the artist, the hidden attraction of a spiritual principle is that it allows a co-creative force to assist with the artmaking.

In the vital areas of creative conduct principles lend meaning, increase focus, and in the midst of difficulty or complications offer clarity and maybe even enlightenment. In art the universal elements and principles of design offer visual guidance. In life (the "big" art) the universal values and principles of living are invisible but nonetheless purposeful.

We've already examined some key values. Now let's explore four principles.

**Principle of Flow**—The most coherent component of the universe is energy. Organized around configurations that are both positive and negative, this energy (i.e. the universe) is constantly being exchanged and everything that we feel and see is an extension of this exchange. By aligning ourselves with this profound phenomenon we can partake of its boundless potential and experience the joy and creativity we seek.

The energy we send out we receive back in kind. Which explains why this principle goes by different names such as *reciprocity, karma, the law of cause and effect*. Whatever it's called, the interconnected energies flowing around and through us influence the harmony in our lives. When we express gratitude, bliss, or love, for example, we not only attract the same in return but often receive it in increased measure. Our giving and receiving in life supports a flow of energy that is expansive in its coming and going.

By giving of ourselves we give to ourselves, thereby increasing our creative flow and attracting creative opportunities as well as any number of other positive possibilities.

*A man there was they called him mad.*

*The more he gave the more he had.*

JOHN BUNYAN

**Principle of Manifestation**—We manifest what we envision and attract what we focus on. What we achieve in life is a reflection of our own will. Everything we attract is there to sustain us in accordance with our goals. The clearer and more meaningful our objectives become in our heart and mind, the easier it is for us and the universe to manifest them on the physical plane.

Our visions have the power to form the realities of our future. For artists they are the seeds of creative change. In fact, as an energizing link between our spirit and the world they are a creative part of everything mankind has made. A vision is both a starting point for a creative journey and a road map for reaching a desired destination. It is needed to not only direct our artmaking but to initiate it as well. In the same way that we manifest success in our lives, the details of our visions empower us to make self-directed and meaningful works in clay.

Frank Saliani, *Analogous Radial*

Velimir Vukicevic, *The Plate*

*All manifestations of art are but landmarks*
*in the progress of the human spirit toward*
*a thing but as yet sensed and*
*far from being possessed. . . .*

ROBERT HENRI

**Principle of Abundance**—We inhabit an abundant universe. Everything we encounter and live through is a natural reflection of the universe's wealth. For this infinite abundance to reveal itself to us we have to first acknowledge that our abundance is not separate from us but at one with us. As we come to accept the spiritual power of this oneness we realize that our spiritual consciousness is our co-creator together with our mindset in determining our prosperity. We are literally the self-expressive force of our own abundance and our abundance projects itself as a productive extension of self. We then have to take the practical steps necessary to manifest thoughts into the physical realm. It's not just an issue of knowing or doing but also a matter of doing something with what we know matters. In the realm of creative activity and abundance we don't need to wait for someone's OK as no one else can do this for us. If we don't do it for ourselves nothing will happen. Ever.

What we think about is generally what comes about. By programming what takes place our thoughts attract what we desire, but the fullness of that experience is hindered if our actions aren't also in supportive alignment with our thinking.

*Life is a mirror and will reflect back to the thinker*
*what he thinks into it.*

ERNEST HOLMES

*Spiritual Principles*

117

**Principle of Nonattachment**—When I was an undergrad one of my non-art professors was particularly taken by a prized work of mine. Twice I refused his offer to purchase it. His third offer, which also went unaccepted, came in the form of a check with the amount left blank. I could have filled in any reasonable price, but I was simply too emotionally attached to the work to let it go. Thinking at the time that such a level of success might not be repeated, I was unable to renounce my uncertainties and clear the way for even greater achievements with clay.

Although I finally did manage to surrender control of my need to keep the piece (selling it years later at an art fair for a lower price to someone less appreciative), I had been nonetheless victimized and manipulated by my own creation. I have since come to realize that every attachment that I have reflects how I feel about myself and that I can enjoy my life more fully when I haven't consigned a lot of rationalized needs to it.

All of us are subservient to anything we have an attachment to: a need, a tradition, a behavior trait, a belief, a relationship, etc. Anything that we relinquish our control to places us in a compromising position—a position of compliant accommodation. Holding on to specific attachments for some sense of personal completeness may actually inhibit fulfillment by blocking the natural flow of the universe's energy and abundance.

Nonattachment is creative freedom. To have the freedom to create openly without limitations, detachment is a necessity. In fact, the very essence of designing requires that we be willfully and freely able to express our desires without anxieties, doubts, or fears. Desires, when not attached to needs, are desirable. They generate energy and advance the creative process forward. Once detached from judgmental needs, we're able to accept things as they are and recognize ourselves as the true creators of our self-worth and not prisoners or slaves of circumstance.

L. Molnar Zsuzsanna, *I Live In You*

Kenneth Baskin, *Connections*

*By letting it go it all gets done. The world is won by*

*those who let it go. But when you try and try.*

*The world is beyond the winning.*

LAO-TZU

As a universal truth of humanity art connects us all. Our unspoken understanding of the visual dynamics of design and of one another on a shared spiritual level allows us the opportunity to communicate through a complex blend of aesthetic experiences. Clay is neutral. It undergoes a fundamental change and becomes art when its form comes from genuine expression and a spirituality that embraces the whole of life.

# PART III

# Design Relationships in Clay

*Design in art is a recognition of the relation between*
*various things, various elements in the creative flux.*
*You can't invent a design. You recognize it, in the fourth dimension.*
*That is, with your blood and your bones, as well as with your eyes.*

D. H. LAWRENCE

# Essential Elements of 3-D Design

What follows are the more or less tangible essentials of the creative process that put the jigsaw puzzle of designing ceramics together. Each distinct formal element is a commanding force unto itself. Individually every one of them is capable of communicating enormous amounts of information, but when put together into an interactive affiliation with one another they quickly form dynamic new relationships. In this way designing takes on new dimensions and higher levels of visual energy. Together these elements enliven our clay and creatively reference the unbounded splendor of ceramics as art.

*What is design? A plan for arranging elements in such a way as to best accomplish a particular purpose.*

CHARLES EAMES

The elements that form the grammatical structure of design language are indispensable mechanisms for generating all aesthetic possibilities in the visual arts. These essential elements are the nonrepresentational, nonsymbolic building blocks of nearly all works of art. In many ways they are similar to *The Periodic Table Of Elements* that lists the essential chemical elements of the universe (90 of which are said to exist within the human body). From these basic chemical elements all other molecular compounds are formed. In chemistry as in design, when two or more different elements are combined the resulting properties are unlike those of its base components.

Within themselves each of these design elements possesses an energy force and each is capable of giving life to our clay. Just as creative energy is life, life is creative energy. In creating ceramic designs we create energy for ourselves and for anyone else who is attracted to the energy of our work. If we use the enormous power of these elements in a fresh and personal manner (mindful of the silent energy of our own truth) then others can respond accordingly and our designs will emit energy in the desired direction. If we compare designs to poetry each compositional element is a word; and we all know how important the choice and placement of a single word of poetry can be to the directed truth (or outcome) of a poem and the influence it might have on others.

As is often the case, we all have conscious or unconscious attractions to specific elements and a tendency to favor one over another. This is very natural and definitely okay as long as the rest are held in esteem and there is no insecurity on our part in utilizing them when appropriate. Henri Matisse cherished the elements of *color* and *shape* whereas Jackson Pollock prized *line* and *movement*. Ceramists too rely on certain elements to carry their work forward. In many instances it is merely a reflection of an individual style or aesthetic preference. Yet whatever the reason, visually resolved designs must maintain an aesthetic balance between the various elements and in doing so contribute to the overall harmony of the work. The artistry of design is physically and spiritually beautiful, but a brilliantly solid design is seldom exclusive.

# 9

# Line

A line is a mark that has length and indicates direction. On flat surfaces its width can appear as thin and delicate as hair or wide and thick like tire tracks. Carved into surfaces, incisions have width plus depth. In space they become linear shapes that illustrate the three dimensions of length, width, and depth.

Lines are the most basic of design elements. Found everywhere in the world of art, they are a versatile element whose expressive contributions seem limitless. To their credit, lines can be full of surprises. One bold scratch, one score from a wooden tool, or one directed smear of colored slip can reconfigure a work of clay. Yet not all lines are so clearly defined. Vagueness often prevails as certain lines, in point of fact, do not exist in our physical world. Some are visually implied and mentally suggested. Without giving visual evidence of their composition they can be the result of a contrast in value or the suggested intersection of planes. There are many ways in which they appear ambiguous—at once seen and unseen. We can be somewhat conscious of their presence as they address our imagination but at the same time we are left with no plausible or conclusive reality to consider or respond to as "line" per se. Nonetheless, lines engage us in a multitude of ways as they visually enrich form and extend the emotional range of feeling.

*Lines, like music, create potential for mystery.*

LINDA SACCOCCIO

The use of lines on clay can be every bit as compelling as they are on paper, even if they aren't used by ceramists as often as by those who work two-dimensionally.  Still, as decoration people have been using lines to embellish clay for thousands of years. Long before lines were beautified with color and painted onto clay surfaces they were carved or etched into the work. In some cases they were used as drawings to tell stories or record events. In others they appeared more abstract and were used expressively. As a means of communication, lines can graphically express all kinds of feelings. Depending on their shape and movement they can have a calming effect and lend a mood of grace and splendor or they can jazz things up with a lively pulsation of reggae-like rhythms.

In many ways lines are extremely symbolic. Straight vertical lines, for example, signify poise and stability while those used horizontally appear relaxed and peaceful. On the other hand, diagonal, zigzag and saw-toothed lines come across as being very forceful. They have a powerful presence capable of generating a vigorous

Rudy Autio, *Apple*

mix of agitation and excitement. This type of dynamic releases vast amounts of energy and denotes anything but a mood of tranquility.

On a more serene level some ceramic artists use line to create shapes on metaphorical forms. Artist Rudy Audio uses soft flowing lines to define or outline shapes that add figurative definition to his clay, but more than anything they provide areas to which he can freely add fields of color. Lines used to delineate the outer boundaries of shapes are commonly called *contour lines*. Although contour lines are generally used to reference the edges of two-dimensional shapes they can also be used to descriptively depict the corner edges of three-dimensional forms. Forms can also share a common edge. When they do they produce physical lines that give added definition to clay. Unlike implied lines which are literally nonexistent yet visually formed in the mind's eye, edges exist as real lines.

The ability to experience the sensual pleasure of lines and to take emotional delight in their movement not only fosters a stronger respect for their function as a potent force in the world of design but it also goes a long way in establishing a more user-friendly relationship, one that comes together to make lines a more fulfilling facet of our artmaking activities. Lines don't necessarily have to show up on every work of clay that we make, but every now and then it's astonishingly enjoyable to be spirited away in the ecstasy of spontaneous line making. Returning to Rudy Audio, one becomes keenly aware while watching him work that he derives more uninhibited enjoyment from the cool, casual carving of lines into leather-hard clay with the tip of a small trowel (his favorite clay tool) than he does from the actual building of his large, hefty sculptures.

Every ceramist seems to have a special capacity for expressive line making, and I cannot leave the subject of lines without paying homage to my wife Gail who among many inborn abilities is one awesome line-maker. The quality of her distinctive line work is conveyed by movement and energy as well as by spirit and wisdom. Her sculptural wall pieces, as diptychs and triptychs, are up to four feet wide and display an array of carved and slip-trailed line configurations. To watch her add these markings to the clay is similar to watching Jackson Pollock paint in that she too uses the natural movement of her entire body, not just her wrist, to bring a living energy to the design.

Prior to the actual physical process of applying lines to her clay, there is a slight energetic shift that she radiates. To someone unfamiliar with her private itinerary for action it may only appear as a momentary pause of silent reflection when in reality she has journeyed inward to unite with the counsel of her spirit to process a meaningful response. Once Gail decides on her approach every cell in her body is seemingly alive with a new vivacity. Infused with life, she literally surges into action and with the immediacy of a dancer she actively applies a myriad of gestural lines across the clay. Although the entirety of this enthusiastic line-making event (from internal coalescence to external completion) occurs in less than a minute's time, each individual line exists as a mark of personal trust and personifies her spiritual identity.

*Once we believe in ourselves we can risk curiosity,*
*wonder, spontaneous delight or any experience that*
*reveals the human spirit.*

E. E. CUMMINGS

People often look to art and artmaking to provide them with the spiritual reserves that science and religion often lack. But I suppose what places spirituality on the cutting edge with creativity is that both already reside within us as a source of energy and a vision for us to express outwardly. Lines and distinctive line-making become a creative extension of these inner visions and when they are allowed

Gail Piepenburg, *Suns of Sabone*

to freely flow from us they open new and compelling pathways to designing in clay. So as artists we need to remind ourselves that lines are energy, an overall extension of our internalized self, and therefore very, very powerful. By doing so our physical use of line will have a defined source of origin and our designs will resonate with more inspiring possibilities.

It is vital that ceramists continue to stake their claim on the use of line to push their work towards new levels of visual communication. Like mortar between bricks, use them to securely hold key elements of a design together within a structural web of coherence. As you work on your line development let me suggest from my own experience that you shy away from what I call the 2-D line which offers less promise and appeal to clay artists than it does to graphic artists in favor of the 3-D line. In addition to having length and width, 3-D lines possess an added dimension of depth that yields new visual experiences of textural relief. The resolution one finds in the use of such multidimensional lines is characterized by their strength of commitment and their ability to integrate themselves within the clay via surface penetration. Scratched, scored, or imprinted, they bring shadow, texture, and an expressive presence to the clay, infusing it with markings of personality and added identity of form.

David Roberts, *Large Vessel With Lines*

# 10

# Form

*The artist must have something to say, for mastery over form is not his goal but rather the adapting of form to its inner meaning.*

WASSILY KANDINSKY

All of us know what form is but do we know what makes it art? Do we know the design context behind its presence, the content behind its meaning? These are issues we need to address as designers and acknowledge as human beings seeking to translate our greater sense of being into art. In this chapter we'll take a look at some of the subtler complexities of form—some human, some physical, and some just plain ambiguous.

Essentially ceramic form is natural clay that has been spiritually charged, humanized, and creatively re-defined as art. The majority of these clay forms are vessel derivative within a more or less functional context. The rest are sculptural. Most of these sculptures are non-objective, exploring relationships between form and space for aesthetic ends. They may or may not address the philosophical views of the artist (as do those that directly reference the figure, architecture, and a host of other interest-specific themes important to individual ceramists), but they may personify them if an artist so chooses because that's what being an artist is about—converting form into something physically and personally compelling. Such sculptures might be blissfully ornamental or they might relate to nature, the environment, history, or culture. Still, regardless of a form's content, form is still form. It has dimensions that define it and the ability to morph both the physical and psychological space it engages.

With this in mind, design's intricate and mysterious power to spatially address form comes into play. If a form's physical and symbolic presence is going to account for anything artistically it must reflect the coexistence between thoughtful design, good craftsmanship and meaningful content. Whether or not design plays the dominant role in this equation is irrelevant. What is important is that it remains a constant fully active presence during the creating process. With any given form I know I'm in the zone if there is at least one magical design moment: a moment of profound and unexpected resolution when the work seemingly exceeds my reach and ends up changing the shape of my world.

*Design is the method of putting form and content*
*together. Design, just as art, has multiple definitions;*
*there is no single definition. Design can be art.*
*Design can be aesthetics. Design is so simple,*
*that's why it is so complicated.*

PAUL RAND

Designing is a problem-defining and problem-solving process that utilizes all sorts of logical skills and analytical talents that originate from the left hemisphere of the human brain, but creative designing doesn't stop there. Not only does it employ the expressive, contextual, and synthesizing components of the right hemisphere, it also utilizes them in concert. For ceramists seeking to bestow expressive verve to ceramic form, this correlation is important to how they design. It is simply not enough to let form follow function as it did in the past without also caring about what the form or object means.

Ceramic form gains visual intensity and expressive uniqueness when it exerts an immediate emotional pull on the viewer. This force comes from seeing what one finds to be appealing and from the narrative it delivers. The narrative, or interface story, keeps the design from being overly stylized and superficial. It introduces an element of energy to form that so many designers and design movements have been unable to recognize. For example, the radically simplified designs originating from the Bauhaus art school (one of modern design's most influential forces) lost their energy edge when they became too fashionable and industrialized—when they promoted tailored efficiency over transcendent thought.

*The use of the term art medium is, to say the least, misleading, for it is the artist that creates a work of art not the medium. It is the artist in photography that gives form to content by a distillation of ideas, thought, experience, insight and understanding.*

EDWARD STEICHE

The clay forms that excite us do not come from mathematical structures, market analysis, technical efficiencies or straight linear thinking. They come from the profound ingenuity of the right hemisphere: from seeing a larger, more humanized picture. As a medium and an art form, clay has a long history of personal relevancy in the human value chain—perhaps more so than any other creative discipline. Technical skills and routines were always a part of its historical development, but not to the detriment of the creative spirit. Forms that express the intricacies of human emotion and personalized thought have often been a product of the design process because right brain work is about doing things one has a passion and a love for. It is this very same passion that motivates people to demonstrate their humanness: to design, to create, and to share their stories.

*The essence of all art is to have pleasure*
*in giving pleasure.*

MIKHAIL BARYSHNIKOV

The challenge for us as ceramists is not to become automatons and repeatedly do those things that ultimately drain life from clay's appearance, but rather to comprehend our human qualities and attentively work them into every form we construct. Because most of us have chosen to work with clay for personal reasons the challenge is not as difficult as it might first seem. Out of our love and excitement for ceramics it is fairly easy for us to bring any number of human intangibles (empathy, inquisitiveness, zeal) to our innovations. These attributes naturally inspire us to stretch our designs beyond the known and seek out forms of intention where little of value is overlooked. As we do so we begin to grasp the power of design to humanize form and soon we realize that in giving form to clay we create an untouchable connection to living that moves us.

It is through this primordial act of meaning that form exists as a primary design element, because every time we give shape to clay we've given shape to our humanism. For ceramists, creating form is a primal act of self-acknowledgement as well as a significant act of communicating with others. Through the visual use of form we bridge gaps between our being and our becoming.

*In every work of art the subject is primordial, whether the artist knows it or not. The measure of the formal qualities is only a sign of the measure of the artist's obsession with his subject; the form is always in proportion to the obsession.*

ALBERTO GIACOMETTI

Most forms are classified as positive forms in that they are solid and occupy space, yet there are also open spaces that are enclosed or defined by positive forms. These contain no material or actual mass and are only created by the positive volumes surrounding them. Such delineated voids, or implied forms, are called *negative forms*. Together these two types of forms bring a physical wholeness and sensual presence to the work via light and shadow. When designing form it is important to remember that empty spaces are every bit as intriguing as the form contours of the work itself. The absence of something can be just as engaging as the existence of something that suggests physical presence.

Ceramic forms can be figurative, representational, nonrepresentational, traditional, experimental, idealized, functional, abstract, or-

Kenneth Baskin, *Union*

ganic, geometric, or iconic—but to be of any real value they need to grow out of the inner intelligence of their designer, secure the attention of viewers, and invite them into a mental, emotional and spiritual experience of their own. What is important to understand here is not just the form itself but the feeling towards it. To shape form we must let go of any perceptions we might hold about it being separate from our feelings. Without this simple distinction our forms cannot attain a sensation of unobstructed oneness with their maker or continue to linger in the hearts of others in the way a great poem or painting does when it is defined by affection rather than approach.

Form is compelling because it both defines and transforms everything we do with clay. Needless to say, the perceptual interplay between our aesthetic sensibilities and our spirituality builds the conceptual framework of the artmaking process and the presence and power of these two transcendent forces are indispensable to form-making.

Many think it is our hands that shape clay when in reality it is our spirit. The process of dealing with form is so highly personal that it impacts our creative vitality. The reason my work in clay is nonrepresentational, at least in the literal sense, is that the overlapping connections between my artistic identity and my spirit direct my expression to those kinds of forms. I personally find my greatest satisfaction and success in creating well conceived and well built forms that are strongly organized around integrated design forces. Object representation or suggestion is not essential to my work, but the way the various parts visually relate to each other in their surrounding space is. By seeking a partnership with design (over allegiance to a process, technique, or complex image) I find that I'm not merely addressing form but creating form with meaning that pre-exists awareness. In this sense my clay work is not only an achievement of design but also a fulfillment of spirit.

Herman Muys, *Untitled Container #47*

# 11

# Space

*We turn clay to make a vessel, but it is in the space where there is nothing that the usefulness of the vessel depends.*

LAO-TZU

Space is three-dimensional. It surrounds everything yet it cannot be seen as much as it can be sensed. Each clay object occupies a specific amount of space, yet the unfilled space it doesn't occupy is also a part of the object—they activate one another. An object's presence can frequently draw attention to its surroundings just as a specific space might invite an object to become an active part of its energy. Clay works with a spatial presence usually have a mystical aura or airiness that extends the sensation of their physical existence beyond the dimensions of their form.

When working out the various aspects of form design, ceramists should account for the overall spatial appearance of their work with

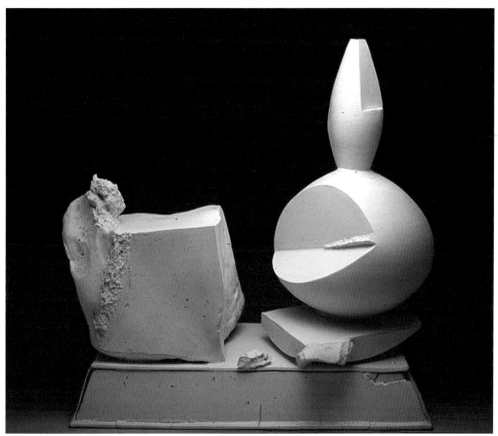

Chris Staley, *Stoneware Still Life*

the same consideration they give to the spatial relationships between various elements on the form's surface—or between multiple forms that together might form a single entity. There are an infinite number of applied forms or surface decorations that can be used to enhance a ceramic object and each one requires a compositional placement decision involving spatial harmony.

*We may say that for the painter space is a luxury; for the sculptor it is a necessity.*

HERBERT READ

Whenever we mount an exhibition of our work we become acutely aware of how each piece is in a spatial relationship to every other piece as well as to its particular location in the gallery setting. In our three-dimensional world all objects interact with one another, with their surroundings, and with their viewers. The aesthetic impact of this reality goes far beyond the mere description of what is happening and should always be addressed on a highly personal level—whether one is an urban planner, architect, or ceramic artist. How the spatial qualities of design affect the human psyche is nothing short of awesome.

*We shape our buildings; thereafter they shape us.*

SIR WINSTON CHURCHILL

Apart from how they might appear, ceramic forms have a relationship with their surroundings that is mutual with regard to their energetic interaction with each other. Form and space enjoy a symbiotic relationship. While it is not possible to view the emptiness of space (as with so many of the larger aspects of nature), there is no doubting the fact that it continuously encircles the clay form, simultaneously responding to it as it in turn responds in kind. This is not unlike the way we acknowledge the surrounding air with every breath taken—knowing that its unseen presence gives us life and allows us to not only feel alive but to be alive.

The concept of spatial significance does not easily correspond to the external aspects of the designing process, but at a subconscious feeling level it's hard to avoid its existence. Space is an unforced presence that does not strive for recognition. It is simply everything the work is not. On the other hand, space is also what the work is about physically, artistically, and spiritually. It impacts the work by penetrating our immediate reality, and by expanding the space within our own minds it allows us to recognize space and the work as one.

*Any great work of art . . . revives and readapts time and space, and the measure of its success is the extent to which it makes you an inhabitant of that world— the extent to which it invites you in and lets you breathe its strange, special air.*

LEONARD BERNSTEIN

As I write these words I'm in South Africa collecting my thoughts after today's visit to the Cape of Good Hope (formerly the Cape of Storms) where the world's highest coastal rock formations and the misty air surrounding them often unite and become

*Space*

145

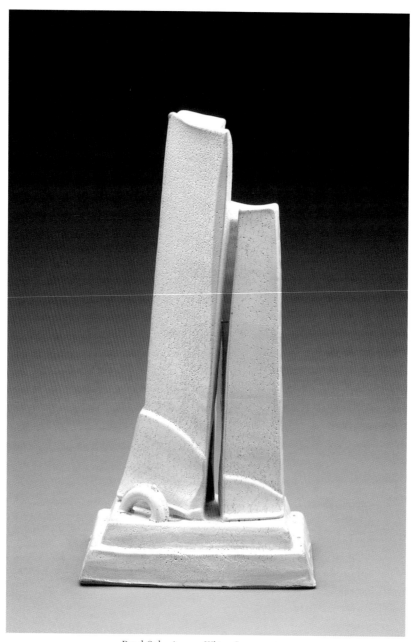

Brad Schwieger, *White Construction*

one in a marriage of separateness. I cannot in the presence of this formidable place with its imposing aura imagine them being independent of one another. Along with the sea they are one. In 1911 the *Lusitania*, like many ships before and after her, was wrecked on those same daunting rock formations I saw just hours ago, not because they were separate entities but because when swathed in fog they became one with the misty air and neighboring sea and were no longer visually distinguishable.

*Space is the breath of art.*

FRANK LLOYD WRIGHT

Space is where artwork lives. Adjoining space can bring life to the art that resides within it or, as in Coleridge's "Rhyme of the Ancient Mariner," it can leave it "stuck, nor breath nor motion; as idle as a painted ship upon a painted ocean." How they affect one another is for each of us to decide. As designers it is our call. Like many things in life, how art influences us and the world we're living in is for us to interpret and to draw individual meaning from. At this level of attended awareness, design touches another level of our lives and becomes a spiritual focal point. Whenever our attention goes beyond the visual or sensual experience of the work and enters a new dimension of our being it allows us to intimately apprehend an altered way of seeing and creating. We need to be attentive to how our creations converge with external forces. By asking whether the spirit of the work mingles with the spirit of the space around it, or even more importantly whether it communes with the spirit of who we are, we can have a fresher sense of what our work is communicating and of our own spatial awareness.

*The idea of space is given to the artist to
change if he can. The subject matter
in the abstract is space.*

WILLIAM DE KOONING

Ceramic form is humanized form and as a testament to the human spirit it not only makes its mark within us but in our space as well. Unfortunately it is all too easy to diminish the capacity for clay to activate the space in which it resides by remaining uncommitted. For example, to varying degrees wheel thrown forms can appear lifeless, restrained by the confines of their very own symmetry. If no compositional components such as lines, textures, or form changes are utilized to visually pull the eye of the viewer around the form, inviting one to physically move about the work and thereby experience its spatial richness, then the completeness of its three-dimensional nature is unrealized.

The French philosopher Joseph Joubert said, "Space is to place as eternity is to time." However right he may have been in defining a contextual reality, with regard to human understanding eternity remains a state of timelessness and space a state of continuousness. Still, the dynamics of space are forever with us and in our uniqueness as designers we may develop ways to artistically embrace both space and time. In architecture, structures create space in a specific place; in ceramics, forms are transformed by the space they inhabit just as much as they change it. Both are space dependent art forms, yet how we design them identifies how they will live in time.

Robert L. Wood, *Twin Span*

# 12

# Color

*Colour does not add a pleasant quality to design—it reinforces it.*

PIERRE BONNARD

Color is everywhere—it's a part of everything we see. It is ordinary but also extraordinary. Thus one of the realities of color is that it embraces a multitude of opposites. It can be light or dark, cool or warm, familiar or exotic. The comparisons are limitless, yet they do not define it. Perhaps its greatest quality, or at least the one that defines it for me, is its ability to immediately awaken our senses and deepen our connection to whatever is at hand. As a stimulant of our world it opens our eyes to new information.

*Mere color, unspoiled by meaning, and unallied with definite form, can speak to the soul in a thousand different ways.*

OSCAR WILDE

Fong Choo, *Tangerina*

Color for a ceramist is not about color theory as it is for a graphic designer or a fine arts painter. It's about *natural color*: the native color characteristics of earth mediums and *applied color*: chemical pigments added to the clay body or to the clay's surface in the formula of a slip or glaze. But more than any of these time honored uses it is also about *psychological color*: the aesthetic control of emotional responses.

Our human response to color arises from experience and the associations it evokes. In a number of ways we're conditioned to relate individual colors to certain emotional sensations: red with passion, yellow with optimism, blue with contemplativeness, and so on. In fact, our intellectual and sensory involvement with color is so strong that we experience difficulty separating a color-descriptive word from the color it's printed in. Try saying the name of the primary color that each of the following words is printed in without actually saying the word itself:

Red Yellow Blue Yellow Red Blue Yellow Red. This is an example of what happens when our visually conditioned response gets confused and loses perspective.

*Color possesses me. I don't have to pursue it.*

*It will possess me always, I know it.*

PAUL KLEE

The reaction that the artist and the viewer are going to have towards the color dynamics of the clay's finished appearance is an integral part of the designing process. Will it evoke an unrefined primitive aesthetic, a spirit of spontaneity, an underlying sense of formality, an ideology, a romantic fantasy, or even a playful response? Our human reactions to clay's surface colors are endless. Nevertheless they need to be assimilated into the designer's mindset if the work is to have any subsequent value as an exchange vehicle for human sensibilities.

As ceramists we eventually come to realize that color, or what we call glaze and surface finish, is the second most significant part of ceramics exceeded in importance only by the forming process. The color may appear on the surface as a stain, underglaze, glaze, or firing treatment, but it is ultimately essential to how the work will be received. In other words, the surface finish is not the finish but rather the beginning, the preparatory ground for the viewer to take their first step toward the storyboard of the work. The finish or color on the clay's surface frames our visual response. If it says "Showtime!" it beckons us forward; if it says "Cancelled" we turn away. If you get this part wrong the dynamics of form are compromised and the work is discounted straightaway. Without the right color treatment on the clay's surface the spiritual vibrancy and essential energies that might have gone into its design and fabrication go undetected and the work literally loses its ability to engage the viewer.

Color is a repository of human emotions. The feelings one has towards a monochromatic color scheme where the colors are closely related values of a single hue (which is a color in its purest state) are much more subdued and subtle than those elicited from multiple color schemes where several colors are juxtaposed. Feelings are even further intensified by contrasting color schemes where colors opposite one another on the color wheel clash and add a vigorous exuberance to a work's presence.

*With color one obtains an energy that*
*seems to stem from witchcraft.*

HENRI MATISSE

Every semester I teach at least one course in basic design where much effort is dedicated to color theory. Why? Because design students generally approach color theory with the same fears and insecurities that my glaze formulation students bring to glaze chemistry. The teacher in me knows that the way we overcome these fears and anxieties in our own lives is through various activities of understanding. By crossing the thresholds of knowledge with uplifted spirits and some basic strategies, I use whatever it takes to turn a trembling handshake (between student and subject) into a firm and self-assured handclasp. My initial strategy for teaching color in a 2-D studio course (though I use many) is to make sure that everyone becomes secure in the acceptance of their own intuition for classifying every color they observe. For example, I make certain that each student has his or her own designation of what true "red" is. The same is done with the middle value of other colors. Without this self-assuredness, uncertainty prevails and hinders innovative judgment.

*Blueness doth express trueness.*

BEN JONSON

The challenges of color identification can be intimidating to say the least and each of us needs the strength of our convictions to think freely about our choices and not be held back by insecurities or confusion. By giving our own meaning to colors we give ourselves permission to creatively move forward and take our glaze experiments in the right direction. One of the personal secrets to the successful use of color (as with enjoying life) is that of maintaining contact with the inner peace of our confidence.

*Colors answer feeling in man; shapes answer thought;*

*and motion answers will.*

JOHN STERLING

One of the colors I have been working closely with that engenders a primordial-like serenity is white. Although white like blacks and grays is technically not considered to be a color but rather a lack of color (a neutral) I personally choose not to view it that way and never could. In undergraduate school where I was a painting major prior to discovering ceramics I remember to this very day one of my respected art teachers not letting us use black pigment because she didn't value it as a genuine color. Justified or not, I acknowledge white and black to be colors—just as I do orange and green—as well as the chromatic grays which I adore.

*White is not the mere absence of color; it is a shining*

*and affirmative thing, as fierce as red, as definite*

*as black. God paints in many colors;*

*but He never paints so gorgeously, I had almost said*

*so gaudily, as when He paints in white.*

G. K. CHESTERTON

My attraction to the color white is fairly recent and a direct result of the evolution of my sculptures. As they began to take on a new potency of form I realized that the color options in my current glaze palette weren't going to complement or adequately represent the maturing strength of the work. I needed a surface finish that was

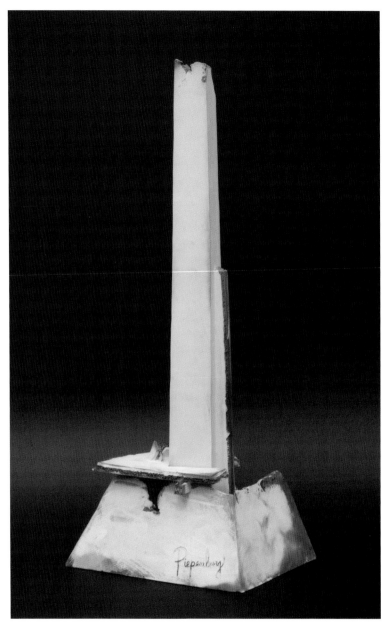

Robert Piepenburg, *Cyrex*

moving in the same direction and at the same speed as the work—hence the color white. I'm still not sure if I chose it or it chose me, but there it was enhancing the subjective intricacies of my constructions without compromising my forms and the materiality of their surface.

*I found I could say things with color and shapes that I couldn't say any other way—things I had no words for.*

GEORGIA O'KEEFFE

The fact is that there is an appropriate color or combination of colors for every design. The forceful colors of a Ron Nagle cup or a Betty Woodman vase would have been way too vigorous a treatment for the aesthetic I was developing. I may have wanted my work to be spellbinding, but in a less assuming rather than spectacular manner.

White may be a nominally subdued color but at the same time it is capable of taking clay work to the brink of an avant-garde sacredness. It's a classic color of originality and freshness—possessing a universal identity of pure, flowing energy. Of course there will always be those who disagree or second-guess one's color decisions, but those decisions are for us to make with each piece we create. Am I saying that the functions of color are crucially important in ceramic art and design? Yes. And I choose the color white for the spiritual dynamic it brings to my work, but had the forms appeared strong and unified on there own without any additional color I could just as easily have left them as they were or I could have simply smoke-fired them. In other words, there is a revealing truth to the fact that ceramic designs don't always require applied color. Consider the example of all those ceramists who accept the unglazed surfaces that the firing process itself wills to them.

*Every form is a base for colour;*
*every colour is the attribute of a form.*

VICTOR VASARELY

Every other semester I teach a second-year glaze formulation class. Students look forward to the second level course with hopes of discovering the ultimate glaze or surface breakthrough for their work. Students in the beginning glaze class, however, are anything but excited. As I've already mentioned, they appear haunted by the unseen apparitions of chemistry and nightmares of their scientific shortcomings. Glaze chemistry can be initially confusing, at least it was for me, but it need not raise any alarms of dread or failure since there are only ten to fifteen basic chemicals that are used to formulate most glaze, engobe, and slip recipes. An average glaze recipe, for example, contains five chemicals, and a low-temperature (cone 05) glaze can even be made from a single ingredient such as gerstley borate or a frit mixed with water. Once the characteristics of each chemical are understood and that knowledge settles in, glaze development becomes an enjoyable activity filled with hope and excitement. From this kind of upbeat starting point a new search for color options can begin, but should the research falter be assured that there are always new ceramics books and websites that contain countless glaze receipts.

Joe Pinkelman, *Untitled*

# 13

# Texture

*The textures that touch us most are those that*
*touch your heart; not your hand.*

AUTHOR UNKNOWN

Texture is a tactile surface quality that visually enhances ceramic form and physically enriches its sensory presence. In two-dimensional design, texture is often used to fill in a shape or background area for contrasting effects, but it is more visual than tactile. This appearance of texture where there virtually is none is often referred to as *apparent* or *implied texture*. For instance, the painted image of tree bark may invoke the irregular feel of rough bark but if the painted canvas were touched the surface would be smooth and featureless. In three-dimensional design the opposite is true. The texture is very real and it can be touched and physically experienced as a tactile sensation.

For the ceramist, texture is an awesome compositional element. No other art medium is more physically receptive to texturing than clay. It yields to the textural imprint of anything we press to its surface. What is equally remarkable is that it also exhibits organic textures of its own. Every time it is stretched, torn, or rolled over onto itself it gives us a whole assortment of textural possibilities, but only if we are receptive enough to accept clay's assistance in the matter.

If one of our functions as the creative designers of our clay work is to follow up feeling with form, it stands to reason that we should also follow up form with texture. If design is the imagination made visible then texture is the imagination made touchable.

*We live amid surfaces, and the true art is*
*to skate well on them.*

RALPH WALDO EMERSON

An appreciation of texture develops naturally and begins by both seeing and touching—two aspects of the tactile experience. First our admiring eye anticipates the journey and then our sensation of touch takes us on tour. The result is that texture becomes a sensation objectified in clay.

The world of textures is infinite. As we come to recognize the value of its contributions it also becomes astonishing. Textures, whether they are natural and intrinsic to the clay or worked and manipulated by the ceramist, can work on a purely physical level, but it's on the aesthetic level that the textured form or surface has real value. Pleasure, joy, excitement, and wonder are not physical things. They are values that our personal emotions and feelings bestow upon the art object. Which is why as we design and fabricate our clay work it is important that we accentuate the relationship that exists between textures and sensory awareness. Otherwise it would be like building an airplane without wings. Not only would it not fly, it wouldn't even get off the ground.

Another use of texture is for contrast. In most instances the quality of a textured area is enhanced when it is experienced in close proximity to a non-textured area. This relationship is important to the overall appearance and definition of the form. Without a balance between these two surface traits the ceramic form is in danger of being weakened and rendered ineffective. There are always instances, however, when just the opposite is true as with Matt Long's ceramic surfaces which are totally covered with a visually delicious coating of heavy slip. Still, his forms enjoy an orderly presence of hardiness and strength that is normally not associated with weighty textures. To once again use the analogy of the airplane, it takes two wings to balance an aircraft in flight. With only one wing a plane couldn't remain airborne. Likewise, texture needs the equilibrium of non-texture. Without this essential balance, design dynamics are destabilized and the visual vitality of a textural presence isn't successful or effective.

> *The moment one gives close attention to anything, even a blade of grass, it becomes a mysterious, awesome, indescribably magnificent world in itself.*
>
> HENRY MILLER

Some ceramic artists create works that are exact visual replicas of existing man-made objects such as Marilyn Levine who creates worn leather suitcases, golf bags, and belts. The textural options for such pieces are restricted to those that best duplicate the actual textures of the original leather. For the rest of us there are an infinite

Elizabeth Lurie, *White on White Teapot*

Tom Phardel, *Union of Two Points*

number of textural options to choose from. We even have the option of creating textures that contradict the character features of the underlying form. This unexpected use of texture is but one of many ways to articulate the incredible possibilities we have at our disposal for detailing our designs and expanding their aesthetic qualities.

*Without texture the union between life and*

*art is incomplete.*

AUTHOR UNKNOWN

While texture appeals to our physical sense of touch and enhances the overall tactile effect of form, it also traps light and creates shadow to produce a sense of contrasting values. These areas of contrast between light and shadow are attractive to the eye. Areas with the brightest or highest value form the highlights and optically serve as focal points for the viewer to begin examining the artwork. The importance of textural/value contrasts to the ambiance of a work of art is easily appreciated in the tactile world of ceramics. Clay works with strong surface undulations often appear quite active, adding supplemental movement and visual enjoyment of the piece, but the real impact of this element is found in its ability to generate an emotional response through variety and contrast. Pleasure, according to Immanuel Kant, arises from sensation. And as those of us who work in clay know, multifaceted surface compositions invoke physical, emotional, and aesthetic sensations simultaneously.

In an art context, texture is a powerful element when it is used to bring attention to specific areas by juxtaposing them with those containing less texture. Characteristically, Gail Piepenburg's large wall reliefs employ limited areas of dramatically gestured textural motifs that are creatively interfaced with smoother, quieter surfaces of clay. Because of the contrast between empty surface and filled surface, the resulting impact of tactile effects is greater and the sensory value dynamics are anything but subtle.

For the artist it is psychologically difficult to walk away from an empty surface and refrain from transforming it, even in some small incremental way. Such reactions are not limited to artists, even though we may have an uncommon need for expression. The term *cenophobia* is used to describe individuals who have an unconscious or irrational fear of empty rooms. In the world of art the Italian term *horror vacui* is used to refer to an artist who cannot refrain from covering the entire surface of his or her artwork with an excessive amount of texture or decorative detailing. Whether such overzealousness results from anxieties associated with empty space or is an intentional form of stylistic expression, it can diminish the overall presence of the surface, suppressing the textural integrity of any one specific area and denying its visual dominance. For texture to have focal value and be an effective visual force it needs to appear uniquely special and it should be used sparingly if it is going to have a visceral effect on the interest of the viewer.

Meira Mathison, *Two Cruets and Tray*

# 14

# Light

*Light and rational forms are locked in combat; light sets them in motion, bends what is straight, makes parallels oval, inscribes circles in the intervals, makes the interval active.*

PAUL KLEE

Light along with shadow gives grandeur, definition, and limitless drama to everything possessing three dimensions. It is a magnificent element of thought-provoking wonder that brings harmony between the creative reaches of our humanness and the world we inhabit. If you've ever experienced a sense of awe or deep wonder at the setting of the sun over the peaks of mountains or a rocky coastline you've had a glimpse into the very character and influence of light.

Photographers have always been aware of the nature of light and shadow. They have peered directly into the heart of its mystery with every click of their camera's shutter. As ceramists there is much we can learn from photographers in the way that they document the visual effects of light. As sculptors working three-dimensionally not only are we aware of the subtle yet influential effects of light on human emotions, but we are directly involved with it through the formation of shadows that bring convincing life to the texture and surface of clay. Ceramists who are especially sensitive to a viewer's emotional response to the overall physical presence of an object acknowledge the purpose of light as a means of representing form. The fact that ceramic form takes strength from light and mystery from shadow only enhances our appreciation and advances our interest to discover more effective ways of using it creatively other than for the staged shooting of our portfolios.

Light not only merges the various elements within a work of clay but it also unites the work with the space it embodies. Together they both contain a feeling and project a mood that contributes to the character of the work. The impact of light on the geometry of the clay object is no less important than the effect it can have on the ambiance of the space it occupies or the feelings it evokes in the hearts and minds of those who see it.

French Impressionists such as Édouard Manet and Claude Monet were not only acquainted with light, they were passionately dedicated to working with it. Their understanding of light's significance revolutionized painting and produced the single most famous artistic movement in history. One of art's most enduring geniuses, Leonardo da Vinci, valued light in painting but dismissed it in sculpture. In his own words he minimized its importance by saying: "The sculptor must consider only volume, form, placing, movement and repose. He does not have to concern himself with light or shadow, for nature produces them herself in sculptures." True, nature does illuminate sculpture in an infinite number of ever-changing ways, yet it is the responsibility of the sculptor to shape forms and surfaces in such a way as to utilize the light—its intensity, its motion, and its shadow—to best complement the work. In the same way that a dancer choreographs the movement of the dance, the sculptor needs to compose the contours of form and coordinate the placement of light and shadow and activate the work in space. In the absence of effective illumination the work loses its definition and form is displaced by silhouette.

In artwork that is two-dimensional, the artistic drama between light and shadow is more nuanced and gradual than it is with sculpture. Artists working on flat surfaces must rely on variations in value, i.e. the degree of lightness to darkness, to define compositional changes of light. Through value contrast and patterning, slight variations in shading are used to give shape, texture, and depth to various structural elements. In addition to creating the impression of three dimensions, varying values create mood. Low-key values suggest feelings of calmness whereas high-key values can be uplifting and convey lively feelings of excitement. However effectively they may be employed, values are used to create the sensation of light and the illusion of shadow where in reality neither exists.

*I always think of shade as being full of light.*
*That is why I always like to use the word shade*
*rather than light and shadow.*

JOHN SLOAN

There is no shadow if there is no volume of form to impede light. The casting of shadows is substantially unique to three-dimensional form. Those working in two-dimensional media don't have this direct link to light to generate refinement and meaning in the artwork. In the story of *Peter Pan*, Peter loses his shadow when a window suddenly slams shut behind him. Later Wendy sews

Gudrun Klix, *Porcelain Coracle III*

Peter's shadow back on. Fortunately for us as ceramists we don't need a needle and thread in our toolboxes. Window or no window, clay shadows are self-reliant and not subject to loss, only to indifference. The excitement of working in clay is that we can utilize the casting of shadows to visually articulate and charge our work. Light is always available to us to anchor our forms and present them with a certain air of authority. The drama of working with light and revealing its essence in our work is that it opens doorways of meaning that unexpectedly promise a new assortment of interesting possibilities.

How might we do this?

For starters, put a tunnel, a channel, a wormhole or whatever under the base of the work—let the light pass through and let shadow begin its dance of aesthetic enchantment.

Raise it up. There is no reason why a clay work should just squat there on its base like Jabba-the-Hutt when it can be visually and psychology elevated by placing feet, legs, or stilts beneath it. Let the light move in and bathe the base area in a mystical atmosphere of shadow play that helps it acquire a new life all its own.

Add appendages (known as applied designs) to engage light and give shape to shadow. Use larger configurations to build up and activate form and smaller outgrowths to enliven the surface skin of contours. Any tactile detail added to form has the potential to restrict light and liberate shadow. The visual value and enhancement of these two interactive forces is not a by-product of our learning as much as it is the realization of an effect that often reaches far beyond our everyday thinking. Our best work may never have consciously included the concept of light as we seldom acknowledge its implications during the design process unless we're constructing with translucent porcelain, but it has often articulated our forms and aptly endowed them with a spatial dynamic more honest and dramatic than we might otherwise have achieved without it.

Maria Eitle-Vozar, *Card House WI*

# 15

# Time

*Time does not become sacred to us until we have lived it, until it has passed over us and taken with it a part of ourselves.*

JOHN BURROUGHS

What multifaceted phenomenon could be more enigmatic than time? Emblematic of all that is truly mystifying (to scientists, philosophers, and artists alike), it permeates life in every way imaginable yet continues to defy human understanding.

The notion of time as a fundamental element of design has yet to reach the aesthetic mainstream of ceramic art. Still, it's a natural presence that influences the physical reality of our work and we'd be resisting innovation if we didn't graciously account for something so profound and let it earn its place, not only in the moment but also in the designing process for work that is yet to follow.

It's been said that "one cannot enter the same river twice," but

Daniel Evans, *Gratuitously Much*

what happens in the past informs that which occurs in the future. Our designs improve and evolve over time, that much we understand. So why can't they progress to another level and be about time?

*Time is not a line, but a series of now points.*

TAISEN DESHIMARU

Within the context of time's passing there are issues that reflect both spiritual and physical truths with regard to ceramics. Still, I've had reservations about introducing and interpreting time's relationship to art (partly because of an aura of evocative mysticism that surrounds it), but I have no doubt about its ability to add significance or to bring relevance to the overall character of clay.

Ceramists have always explored the nature of time's abstract characteristics—some knowingly and some unknowingly. There is a movement in ceramics called *conceptualism*. Conceptualists who work with clay are well aware of their baseline relationship to time. Their work is not so much about form and material as it is about an idea or concept. More often than not they intentionally rely on the passage of time and the elements of nature (sunshine, wind, rain) to transform not only the surface of the clay but the shape of its form as well. Their unfired clay pieces have been exposed to the waves and tides of coastal shorelines and periodically photographed to document the changes that were slowly but naturally occurring. Other clay forms have simply been placed in quiet ponds or containers of still water to be liquidated, transformed into small colloidal particles that end up somewhere in that gap between muddy mess and masterpiece. Still others have been very site-specific, located on window ledges, in stairwells, museums, galleries, or in the baking heat of the desert where they are left to dry under the ripening rays of the sun, to shrink and crack—giving the grace of time full reign.

As a rakuist I've always been attracted to raku-fired clay in part because of the timeless nature of its surface and a myriad of subtle qualities that visually transcend time and raise questions of *when* and *where*—was it made recently or a thousand years ago and where did it originate?

The timelessness of a ceramic surface can transcend the present moment and take us to other places and periods in time. It can allow us to feel and experience all kinds of human qualities from joy and gratitude to admiration and desire. In short, it can become a central aspect of one's work. If we direct attention to the number of ceramists who have chosen to design their work around a firing process it quickly becomes apparent that a large number have collectively assimilated the hidden energy and power of time's aesthetic contribution.  Just as our muscles become stronger when we use them and our integrity becomes greater when we live with integrity, our clay works more greatly manifest time's ability to be an empowering force the more often we make use of it in the design process. It's not a coincidence that such a large number of individuals working in clay today prefer to wood-fire, smoke-fire, or use other primitive firing techniques so that the surface of their work captures a place on time's palette, reflects a glimpse of history, or psychologically references idealized images of another place and life somewhere in time.

*They say that time changes things, but you actually
have to change them yourself.*

ANDY WARHOL

Philosophical theories of time may not have predated mankind's use of clay but they do at least date back to Aristotle and St. Augustine who believed that time exists only in our apprehension of reality. It has even been suggested that Einstein's theory of relativity shows time to be subjective or observer dependent. His theory asserts that the measurement of an event's duration isn't absolute but relative to an observer's frame of reference. Together these theories set the stage for a set of distinctions separating physical time from psychological time with some issues requiring quantitative scientific examination and others qualitative philosophical analysis.

*The aim of art is to represent not the outward*
*appearance of things, but their inward significance.*

ARISTOTLE

Philosophers, like artists, address intuitions—their own as well as ours. The Frenchman Henri Bergson claimed that intuition is "deeper" than intellect. In 1927, Bergson received the Nobel Prize for Literature and in his work *Time and Free Will* made the distinction between mathematical time and pure time. He maintained that mathematical time is of a measurable duration, consisting of explicit intervals, while pure time consists of a real or true duration that is a continuous and non-divisible flow of experience that can only be recognized intuitively. For Bergson, intuition as a fluidity of psychological activity versus a single act exists beyond intellectual concepts and is a direct insight or encounter with the makeup of reality.

Whatever time is or isn't, it does bring us face to face with our own intuition. And if the intellect does have a propensity for falsifying our perceptions of reality as Bergson claims, then intuition as a form of knowledge can be utilized to complement our clay work by revealing what is real and what is possible—whether in relationship to time or to any other aspect of reality.

*Intuition is the super-logic that cuts out all*
*the routine processes of thought and leaps straight*
*from the problem to the answer.*

ROBERT GRAVES

To work with the element of time we need to take the time to see how the dynamics of change might work with our own design process. If we just take time out to explore the variety of sensations surrounding every moment of our existence we might discover new content themes to investigate aesthetically or learn to express a deeper understanding of one of life's marvelous gifts through the three-dimensional use of clay. Life would lack purpose if we simply passed through without taking the time to observe it, engage in it, and with some sense of creative passion share it.

By taking time out to get a closer look at what's around us not only do we observe more but we also expand our ability to take in the key details of the larger picture. Many ceramists have spent a lot of time observing nature—itself a living paradigm of creativity—and have found there a muse for their designs. After having taken the time to listen to music others have discovered new images and design ideas that make their journey with clay more meaningful. Each time we slow down we let our spirit absorb not only sights and sounds but inspirational power as well. Whenever we make the time to find a sense of sacredness in various aspects of our life we are using time to awaken our creativity while at the same time becoming aware spiritually of any greater purpose it might hold for us. If, as an exercise, we took an extended period of our time to study a single piece of fruit (such as a pear) or listen to a single piece of music (without vocals, as words can take control of our imagination) and immediately transfer the force of our experience to clay, what new responses or discoveries might emerge and contribute to our design process?

Gudrun Klix, *Night Journey*

*Nothing valuable can be lost by taking time.*

ABRAHAM LINCOLN

In reality time never stands still. But we can figuratively stop its movement (in the same way a photograph can) by freezing an image, a feeling, or an intention in clay and conveying the impression metaphorically of its existence in another dimension of time. A good example of this would be the amazing replications of old worn leather products in Marilyn Levine's clay works. Not only do they fool the eye (*trompe l'oeil*) but they transport our perceptions to a former place in time.

Each of us has memories of times and events that are of great personal value, especially those that moved us to alter the course of our lives. Creative people have always traveled back in time to seek the inspirational influences of a past narrative and to re-create something in the present that is capable of touching the human spirit in a way that is as evocative now as it was then. In art, facets of time are always present. The challenge is to view them in a way that makes memories and experiences purposeful as we push our work towards the future.

In and of itself time is an emergent entity in the same way designing is an emergent process. What connects them and what adds to the complexity of their future contributions to aesthetic possibilities is the identifying knowledge of our own experience. Over time this natural knowingness changes what we think and as our thinking changes so do our creative responses. By allowing us the opportunity to more fully comprehend our experiences, time becomes a structural component of creativity and an evolutionary link to our design sensibilities.

Margaret Boozer, *In Your Own Backyard*

# Organizational Principles
of 3-D Design

Design principles are the structural means used to organize the formal elements of design. Through a process of selective integration they bring the various compositional elements into a visual wholeness. They are not recipes or formulas. They are neither conditional nor restrictive, nor are they unequivocal or absolute. They are simply instructional guides and as such they have been universally developed and used over centuries to provide aesthetic direction to the design process. Their utilization is the hallmark of a great design.

*What seems to divide the excellent and lasting*
*from the mundane and forgettable works*
*is the underlying design control . . .*
*this basic abstract organization of elements.*

RON RANSON

The organizational principles of design, more so than the elements, are dependent upon our philosophical approach to living and artmaking. Creative personalities generally shy away from situations loaded with restrictions and rigid boundaries. The fact is that creative people are known for breaking rules and being unconventional. The rule here might be not to have many rules. Granted, we need to understand the role these principles play but we also need to know when they become too limiting. Just as importantly we need to know our own motivations for doing what we do. If we believe in ourselves and feel comfortable with these organizational standards we can, with a self-realized freedom, constructively apply them when creating works from clay.

There are two distinct attributes we can ascribe to the principles of design: first, they have creative value; and secondly, they create value. Creatively they are valuable in that they give us the freedom to be wholeheartedly expressive in situations of uncertainty. The unknown is territory that can undermine the freedom of any designer, but with the principles of design to guide us our capacity to trust is increased while fears of uncertainty are lessened. And without trust how creative can we be? At the same time design principles create value by offering us an amazing framework for transforming the ordinary into the extraordinary. They can appear exquisitely simple or as complex as life itself. Either way they await our understanding and unlimited use. By utilizing the organizational principles found in the following chapters we enhance the spatial order and compositional enrichment of our artwork and create a whole new reality for our clay.

# 16

# Balance

*What I dream of is an art of balance . . .*

HENRI MATISSE

Balance is the physical as well as visual equilibrium of a three-dimensional design and it is achieved through the harmonious arrangement of its component parts. If works of clay aren't balanced through the proper distribution of weight they are unstable and vulnerable to the risk of falling over. And if they aren't balanced visually they appear awkward and aesthetically unresolved, psychologically leaving the viewer on edge.

There are various ways to categorize different forms of balance. *Actual* or *literal balance* refers to the compositional dispersion of dimensional and material weight. *Symmetrical* or *formal balance* shows both sides of the work as being identical in appearance and weight. *Asymmetrical* or *informal balance* is often more visually dynamic in that the work appears stable by projecting the illusion of balance through compositional organization without the exactitude of duplication. *Radial balance* is the term for a kind of balance that radiates from a central location like the spokes of a wheel. Used in conjunction with a repetitive motif it can be quite effective on large plate forms and wall sculptures in relief.

*The most general law in nature is equity—*
*the principle of balance and symmetry, which guides*
*the growth of forms along the lines of*
*the greatest structural efficiency.*

HERBERT READ

However one feels about balance it plays a crucial albeit subtle function in the aesthetics of a design concept. Balance, like love, is something that is best enhanced in our own life before we can share it with others or bring it to bear on our designs. The English sculptor Barbara Hepworth understood this human phenomenon when she said, "Body experience . . . is the center of creation." Personal poise manifests itself as an unwavering sense of deep inner peace. Balance in design manifests itself as a visual representation of that inner stability. The same is true in dance where the spirit of the dancer lives in the body and is visually expressed in the dance.

The whole of science, said Einstein, is nothing more than a refinement of everyday thinking. The whole of our designs is also a refinement of thinking. If we don't equate our inner balance with the visual balance in our work the result is one-sided and unbalanced. The notion of personal balance applies to everything our life touches, from a range of private, social, and professional

Jayson Lawfer, *Translation of an Important Idea*

interactions to the compositional structuring of a variety of design elements. An unbalanced life may or may not render us dysfunctional, but it's not the healthiest base of support to be designing from.

*Balance is the perfect state of still Water.*

*Let that be our model.*

*It remains quiet within and is not*

*disturbed on the surface.*

CONFUCIUS

As with any difficult aspect of the design process the problem can be with the designer and his or her current limitations rather than the specifics of the design. The design elements may be basic and easily understood but the principles surrounding their implementation can become highly complex in which case it's crucial to recognize how personal issues can put a strain on one's abilities and have a corrosive effect on design decisions. One issue that stands out above all others here is the inability to connect with the inner wisdom of our true self—a self that is deeper than personality. This wisdom is the meaningful core of the spirit, the center of our peace, and the strength of our convictions. By trusting in the truth of our inner voice we release some of the doubts and fears that surround everyday thinking and become productively liberated and capable of not only balancing our designs but revolutionizing them as well.

The practice of assessing personal strengths and weaknesses has strategic parallels to identifying which elements support a balanced design relationship and which ones destabilize its appearance by disrupting the harmony of visual and spatial equilibrium. When ceramists manipulate their shapes and textures they have to constantly assess the positioning, proportioning, and placement of each individual part until everything is situated and spaced in a way that supports the perception of aesthetic coherency. When done successfully the alteration of even one component can disturb its overall sense of poise.

*A rock pile ceases to be a rock pile the moment*
*a single man contemplates it, bearing within him*
*the image of a cathedral.*

ANTOINE DE SAINT-EXUPERY

For a finished work of clay to be in a state of artistic balance it must hold together in space as an inseparable whole. It should stand with believable purpose with all of its negative and positive shapes physically distributed so as to assure a visual stability of weight and form. This mass-void relationship can best be analyzed through the placement of imaginary reference lines or axes. For example, by perceiving a vertical axis at the center of a clay form the eye can determine from all angles whether or not the visual weight is equal on either side. The same, however, is not true with a horizontal axis. Here you want the bottom half to appear more weighted and stabilizing. This approach is obviously made more difficult with asymmetrical forms made up of several interconnected parts. In this case the ceramist might want to visually break the work up into a number of smaller units and after affirming their various centers of balance gradually bring the composition into a balanced relationship of visual unity.

All of us, according to Deepak Chopra, are "infinite choice makers." These choices, both conscious and unconscious, influence our designs as much as they do our daily activities. The physical process of bringing balance to a design is much like the challenge of maintaining one's equilibrium while walking on a log. In the same way that we intuitively make adjustments with our arms and shoulders to keep from falling, we work through a series of design arrangements and modifications to arrive at a sense of visual equilibrium. We establish balance in our designs by combining the different elements so that they counterbalance one another and generate an overall feeling of balanced harmony.

Although hard to comprehend, we intuitively recognize a composition's balance when it is present and, even more importantly, when it is not. If in doubt, ask yourself the following questions: Is the design lopsided, congested, top-heavy, disproportionate, or lacking visual strength? If so, alter the placement relationships between the existing elements by redistributing the attributes of texture, color, proportion, negative space, size, form, and density until the effect is one of visual stability and personal appeal.

A work should ultimately be evaluated and judged to be in balance when it is in sync with the inner equilibrium of our being. For such a decision to be reached there is no right or wrong, no Euclidian *golden section* formula or *rule of thirds* to consult. In the end there is only our own judgment as an artist, designer, and unique sensitive human being in harmony with our own center.

Jim Lutomski, *Winged Bottle Form*

# 17

# Movement

*The aim of every artist is to arrest motion, which is life, by artificial means and hold it fixed, so that a hundred years later, when a stranger looks at it, it moves again since it is life.*

WILLIAM FAULKNER

Whenever the principle of movement comes to my attention I invariably find myself envisioning the rhythmic fluidity of Vincent van Gogh's drawings and colorful paintings. Although he is not my favorite painter I seem to magnetically come across his work whenever and wherever I travel. And with each and every encounter I rediscover a visual flurry of motion and emotion that mirrors a universe of feelings that are hard to ignore. Vincent (as he preferred to be called) expressed a radically unique approach to movement and in doing so he managed to instill his art with an emotional/psychological form of kinetic energy that appears timeless, both in its influence and in its expressions.

Not every work of clay that we orchestrate needs to reflect the radiant activity of a Van Gogh *Starry Night*, but it should possess at least some fluidity of movement. If we too hope to make artworks of substance and vitality that result from the freedom of movement our spirits are able to exercise during their formation then we need to achieve a heightened understanding and appreciation of visual movement as a lively contribution to compositional value.

*The sense of motion in painting and sculpture*
*has long been considered as one of the primary*
*elements of the composition.*

ALEXANDER CALDER

In the visual arts how we generate the illusion or suggestion of motion matters because it affects the overall magic of a graceful and elegant response that can be if not mesmerizing at least pleasantly alluring. The optical phenomenon of movement is an amazing design tool for energizing ceramic works. Used effectively it gives form an articulate voice and generates a sense of liveliness and high-spiritedness, moving the work from a static state of abstraction to an animated expression of spirited energy. On a more intimate level it catches the eye and attention of the viewer, turning passive observation into responsive action. Depending on how the ceramist arranges the various components of the design's composition, he or she can pilot eye movement along any pathway, at any speed, and thereby direct and delight the viewer's participation.

*Get the art of controlling the observer—*
*that is composition.*

ROBERT HENRI

Eva Hild, *Working in the studio*

The visual kinesis of sculpted movement differs from actual movement. The liveliness that we associate with real-time motion as a verifiable part of our everyday life has to be designed into clay works if they are to impart a visual vibrancy that matches the dynamism of real life occurrences. Induced movement occurs in three-dimensional work when its structural variations are placed in a sequential relationship to one another through sinuosity, patterning, or some form of successive repetition.

In design a lot of what is equated with movement is referred to as rhythm—the repetitive recurrence of compositional components. While visual rhythm relies on repetition, repetition alone doesn't establish rhythm. The repeated uses of geometrical motifs, horizontal elements, or vertical components rarely contribute to compositional movement in the way organic or diagonal features do. A similar comparison can be made between designs that are formally and informally balanced with the former lacking any sense of movement or energy, appearing still and lifeless as if frozen in time.

Rhythm as an exceptionally lively aspect of movement can be used to elicit many of the same emotional responses as music, including some little dance moves we find ourselves doing after a super successful design maneuver with the clay. Just as musical rhythms with their structural patterning of durations between beats create sensual energies for the ear, visual rhythms create lyrical energies for the eye. And when both sensations happen simultaneously . . . wow! The here-and-now becomes a paradise.

*Rhythm is as necessary in a picture as pigment;*
*it is as much a part of painting as of music.*

WALTER J. PHILLIPS

Rhythms in artwork and in music rely on the interconnections between similar sets of components. One set is apparent to the eye, the other to the ear. Art and music are both made by the regular repetition of like elements and the organization of the spaces between them. For further enhancement the size and/or shape of similar elements can be progressively increased or decreased along with the durations of their respective spacing in order to augment their aesthetic potential. In music the pitch is altered; in ceramics it's the shape. If both were to remain constant (like a monotonous percussionist beat or monolithic wall of clay coils) we'd end up with a form of monotonic patterning that might best be broken up with intervals of silence or surface smoothness. Through careful spacing and positioning, major and minor variations are established as well as dominant themes and areas of emphasis.

Works of both art and music contain themes and variations on those themes and next to repetition variety contributes the most to the visual energy of clay work. By alternating (in systematic and coherent arrangements) textured areas with non-textured areas, small shapes with larger shapes, or any of the design's other elements with an opposing characteristic, we create additional visual interest. Variety creates contrast and contrast increases the rhythmic dynamics of compositional forces by highlighting their directional movement. Strong contrasts can energize the rhythmic pace of a design and operate as lively purveyors of visual excitement that the active eye of the observer is drawn to. Subtler contrasts like the repetitive placement of similar elements at more predictable intervals smoothes out the rhythmic pace and slows eye movement.

*Movement can often make the mediocre magnificent.*

ANONYMOUS

In addition to influencing our emotional responses to artwork, rhythm and movement regulate our visual journey around the work: setting our speed, mapping our turns, locating our rest stops and directing us to destinations of interest. To make this trip worthwhile and enjoyable for the viewer we as ceramists have to use our design skills with the highest level of creative attentiveness, for it is our humanness in tempo with our spirit that reinforces our creativity and allows it to flow with greater ease.

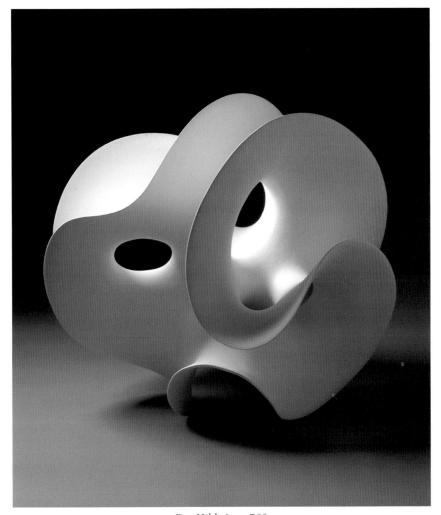

Eva Hild, *Loop 785*

18

# Unity

*There are points of time, of distant memory, when the soul*
*unites within the pattern of the universe. That union*
*brings forth the understanding of life's harmony.*

AUTHOR UNKNOWN

For me the concept of unity is one of the most potent principles of successful design because it brings the various essentials of a work together and fuses it with a sense of wholeness.

Without unity designs can appear visually  D i S o R d Er e D and **C** ha o t ic. When lacking qualities of togetherness a design can appear dysfunctional and show little evidence of intention.  Of course there is such a thing as overdoing it when there is too much sameness and the various details of the work end up becoming overly stylized and monotonous. But without some sense of unity there is no unfolding or achievement of control, order, planning, or even more importantly a oneness of purpose.

Whenever possible it is important for the ceramist to design with purpose. The ambiguous placement or grouping of disconnected parts leads to viewer confusion in the same way that an unintended area of focus or emphasis can muddle the designer's intent and rob a work of its power as a visual entity.

In many ways designing is a reflection of our desire that we bring to our clay, not just to manipulate its form but also to activate experiences for ourselves as well as others. Although designs in and of themselves are not reliable carriers of meaning (for that we're better off examining the expressionistic and subjective nature of the work's original source imagery), they do arouse our awareness and prompt us to act and embrace our human potential. In doing so we invariably become consciously at one with our perceptions. In this way good designs go beyond their physical appearance and influence the wholeness of our existence.

In principle unity may have little to do with an artwork's meaning, but in practice it both supports and refines it. Our designs are attributable to our imagination, and while our imagination doesn't always provide us with an initial illustration of how we can best grace our work with the visual orderliness it needs to survive, it does play a role in helping to bring things together. Along with the inner workings of our being (our intellect, thoughts, and emotions) our imagination—which is also a reflection of spiritual sensations—helps locate the pieces so that they interact in an orderly fashion and interrelate as a natural and harmonious whole.

*Inspiration is a moment of contact with another reality,*
*the moment when everything at once falls into its proper*
*place, when as it were, the entire structure appears, and*
*every part is seen to be related to the whole.*

ILONKA KARASZ

Benjamin Carter, *Juice Glasses on Tray*

It is through our sense of personal unity that we become more attuned to the complex connections between parts and the richness of the whole. It's what brings forth multiple design contexts (including a series of forever unique choices in response to the particular needs of the artwork at hand) from which a more inclusive wholeness might emerge. As we gain a deeper understanding of our own generative process we become more adept at identifying the conditions, strategies, and mindset needed to resourcefully adapt such insights to the design process.

With this in mind I should add that one of my own favorite compositional principles is repetition. With its ability to create coherence it is an almost foolproof resource when it comes to linking parts together and weaving them into a relational whole. The repetition of common elements such as parts organized or grouped together in a thoughtful versus haphazard manner can be one of the most successful strategies for bringing wholeness to a work's design. How each of us chooses to use this technique is a personal response to the challenge at hand. I only know that it has to arise jointly from personal thoughts and feelings to visually add subjective value to an otherwise objective form.

*Repetition is the reality and the seriousness of life.*

SOREN KIERKEGAARD

The organizational demands of every design are different but the need for a harmonious state of existence is essential. To achieve wholeness and bring a sense of continuity to each of our clay works we have to constantly contemplate and reconsider every artistic action or technique used. We have to ask ourselves: Are all of the parts in proportional harmony to one another and to the work as a whole? Does a harmonic sense of balance exist between the scale of primary and secondary forms? Are the repetitive elements static or do they emit rhythmic pulses of visual energy? Do distinctive contours and edges connect with the compositional forces around them? The list is long but the objective remains constant: to achieve an overall sense of aesthetic unity.

Unity is the phenomenon that holds things together. It defines and maintains structural continuity and through creative processes it can produce aesthetic designs that convey a unifying condition of wholeness. Simply put, unity generates wholeness. And because it plays the same interactive role in art as it does in life it is fitting that we also be aware of its function as a conduit for the senses in synchronizing the unfolding elements of our life.

*Science is organized knowledge.*
*Wisdom is organized life.*

IMMANUEL KANT

As human beings we're all part of a holistic universe. We are co-creative participants in the whole of life and we all have an effect on it, however small. If we consciously recognize the near and far influences of our involvement hopefully we'll also become responsible participants in caring for the whole of our world. On a more personal level what's creatively important to us as designers is that we tend to the numerous facets of our own existence and find communion with those fragmented elements of self, working and living from a more harmonized place of individual completeness. If we can manage a more art-conscious existence and live in the orderliness of our own unification we will be better able to embody the dynamics of unity in our work. In doing so we'll see that the wholeness within our lives becomes the formative force of wholeness in our actions. In a sense the creative continuity within any given design is an incarnation of the artist's personal synergy.

*Individuality is only possible if it*
*unfolds from wholeness.*

DAVID BOHM

As ceramists we know not to touch hot kiln bricks or hot pieces of pottery fresh out of the kiln. In the same way we've been taught not to touch places inside ourselves that are too hot to handle either emotionally or psychologically. But when we're designing and creating with clay we're somehow able to go beyond such conditioned limitations and not only lay a hand on the best of what's inside of us but possibly express something that's even greater than who we are. This is what enriches our clay work and our spirit. This is why we design and it's what gives creativity its significance, spirituality, and sacredness. To the degree that wholeness resides within each of us it also inhabits what we do. Artists know that while their lives are not without restrictions the wholeness of who they are is always free of creative limits and full of hopeful possibilities. Our wholeness, our personal state of union and oneness, is perhaps the highest achievement of humanness we can strive for. It alone processes the various realities of our life and transforms them into higher visions for living with a greater connection to the natural order of what matters.

*. . . and the thousands of fishes moved as a huge beast,*
*piercing the water. They appear united, inexorably*
*bound by common fate. How comes this unity?*

AUTHOR UNKNOWN

# 19

# Variety

*Variety is the condition of harmony.*

THOMAS CARLYLE

Variety is what holds entities together while at the same time making them more fascinating.

Designers, like architects, film directors, dance choreographers, or for that matter just about anyone who is passionately involved with the design aspects of their work, utilize an interactive relationship between the concepts of unity and variety, both of which are major design principles juxtaposed on the same organizational arc of visual order. Where unity strives for a sense of commonality to bring parts into an orderly whole, variety is used to achieve a sense of disorder—but in a uniquely coherent and orderly manner.

Variety contributes to wholeness through organizational arrangement and thematic relationship. In design it serves to put for-

Anthony Caro, *The Moroccans*

ward fresh and successive modifications of the work's foundational premise while visually integrating them into its overall theme. At first this may appear to be a contradiction (achieving structural harmony through a process of divergent changes) when in fact harmonization does occur.

This is especially true when these changes are varied to the extent that they significantly rework or repeat the theme while not departing from it in an unrecognizable way. In music, variation is also a fundamental compositional device. Variations on a leading melody (which may serve as the musical theme) occur through repeated versions of that melody, each of which has been varied by significant changes in rhythm, harmony, or scale. Such insertions of major or minor artistic variations into the thematic framework of art and music expand the final impact of the work. They also represent compositional organization at the highest levels of inspired understanding.

*The moment at which music reveals its true nature*
*is contained in the ancient exercise of*
*the theme with variations. The complete mystery of*
*music is explained right there.*

PIERRE SCHAEFFER

Ceramists have a tendency to become so engaged with their medium that they overlook the importance of design and the critical thinking needed to process vital organizational principles (such as variety) to achieve visual and structural unification. Many of us came to clay through our senses and passions so it's not that unusual to remain wrapped up in the physical marvel of the making rather than attend to a complex configuration of design relationships. But sooner or later after the physical memorization of various techniques and the production of numerous forms we're faced with an acute desire to convey a nobler sense of order with our time and our clay.

Through design the ceramist brings a sense of completeness to the plasticity of the clay—a conceptual wholeness to its structural identity. When the dissonance from a variety of forms or textures is utilized to attain such a transformation the stabilizing forces of balance, rhythm, and unity can become strained and the compositional order visually stressed. But by no means is this state of visual tension a bad thing. There is a great deal of interest that can be generated from the effects of tension. If variety as a strategy is not used irresponsibly it can add enormous energy to any work of art. The dynamics between assimilation and rejection, consistencies and inconsistencies, and the clash of opposites can all be charged with newfound vigor. Such vitality is a potent force capable of changing compositional elements into a transcendentally rousing work of art. In design every technique holds the promise of being valuable. It should come as no surprise, therefore, that surface tensions can be used inconsequentially or they can be made to generate feelings of aliveness.

*Nature is an endless combination and repetition of a very few laws. She hums the old well-known air through innumerable variations.*

RALPH WALDO EMERSON

While it is true that too much of a good thing can compromise the dynamics of viewer interest, a scarcity of visual variety can be disorientating to the senses. The variations between large and small

Joe Szutz, *Myth of Invincibility*

shapes, thick and thin slabs, straight and curved contours, smooth and rough surfaces all reconfigure the relationships that articulate the functioning of clay works in space and invite the viewer to become actively engaged in the artistry of what they see before them. In terms of both structure and aesthetics, variety in a work's design helps it to be present in a way that moves beyond the rational functioning of differences to hold viewer attention.

Variety gives artwork its inspirational and visual punch which helps the viewer to seize the pleasures not only inherent in the touch and focus of a clay work but also in the experience of bringing more meaning to their lives. The unfolding of meaning in a work of art can happen suddenly or over time just as variety can support a design with audacity or unpretentious nuances. It is a component of the designer's language and unquestionably contributes to the compositional completeness of the work. If utilized well it contributes to the success of the work by giving the viewer a greater sense of his or her own completeness through the experiencing of it.

*A work of art must carry in itself its complete significance and impose it upon the beholder even before he can identify the subject matter . . .*

HENRI MATISSE

Like a poet who thoughtfully chooses his or her words and skillfully arranges them in relation to the expressive content of other mindfully chosen words, the ceramist working through the discerning choice and placement of various design elements is working to bring a sense of meaning and supportive harmony to the entirety of the work. To do this each element, like each stanza of a poem, is extremely important to the overall task and must address the heartbeat of the work while being neither too overwhelming nor too uncertain.

*No tears in the writer, no tears in the reader.*

ROBERT FROST

Both the designer and the poet know they need to break the rules every once in a while to give what they do a spontaneous dose of meaningful energy. At the same time they know that it needs to be done in a way that is universally understood. Both poetry and design are expressions of our beliefs. For the ceramist who seeks the transformation of ceramic's traditional formatting into transcendentally original works of human substance, design is much more than a set of working principles; it is a revelation of spirit. As such these wonders of human spirituality invite contemplation as physical entities through which others can discover inspiration within their own lives.

Variety in design as in life is a potent source of vitality. By allowing the forces of creativity to burst through the routine (that which is boring, repetitive, monotonous, and predictable) and rouse the imagination, the use of variety becomes a stimulating catalyst both physically and spiritually for attaining new levels of hope and passion. For our own well-being and for our work in ceramics we need to remain open to our gifts of spirit and allow them to contribute to our designs just as we integrate them into the deeper recesses of our lives. If we don't we risk living and creating without personal meaning, but when we have a spiritual connection to self we are able to create ceramic works that are expressively fresh, inspirational, and alive with the unexpected.

Herman Muys, *Troon*

# 20

# Emphasis

*The soul's emphasis is always right.*

RALPH WALDO EMERSON

My colleagues who teach art appreciation frequently use the term *focal point* when explaining the visual workings of art objects. More specifically, they use it to describe that area of the composition that captivates the viewer's interest. As this approach seeks to educate the artistic eye through a detailed breakdown of a work's finer points it invariably strives to identify those compelling features of the work that literally capture our eye and retain our interest.

Actually the focal point need not be a point at all. It can be and often is an area. Focal areas are distinct and specialized places in a composition that draw most of the viewer's attention. As the center of interest they are the *homepage* that the viewer returns to between exploratory visits to other sites (i.e. areas) of the composition. The centripetal nature of focal points is by and large associated with two-dimensional work where it serves as an identifiable vanishing point for directional lines and diagonal edges to point, lead, or converge towards. Ceramists and others who work three-dimensionally typically use the more descriptive terms *focal area* and *emphasis* to expand the concept of a single point. All three terms parallel one another in their ability to denote center and highlight interest.

Like focal area, emphasis refers to an artwork's center of relevant interest. It is the eye-catching center of the work, that area of prominence that is noticed first. As the design's primary focus it conveys the compositional character of the work and like a book's title it suggests the theme of the work. More often than not this area is formed when one element or compositional arrangement establishes itself within a visual hierarchy of importance as the ranking component, the key ingredient that most reflects the strength and purpose of the design's concept.

*Every portrait that is painted with feeling is a*
*portrait of the artist, not of the sitter.*

OSCAR WILDE

The series of tabletop sculptures I'm currently working on are oriented around standing circular forms. The circle as a time honored and universally sacred shape is important to me for its thematic content as an unfolding reflection of creation. Even Jung describes it as being symbolic of the "innermost godlike essence of man." Yet in addition to it being a principle shape with primal characteristics it is the emphasis of my work—the focal context around which the additional pieces of my spatial puzzlers owe their existence. It is instantly apparent to the viewer upon seeing these forms that the

Ana England, *Touching the Earth*

visual dominance of a circular profile is the nucleus or transitional center that presides over the rest of my compositional elements.

Dominance is a visual attribute of emphasis and a condition that is supportive of it. The dynamics of secondary features in relation to a primary entity help all of the elements to bond and work together to achieve a stronger sense of unity. Without a clear center of focus a design may seem to have multiple centers of focus and appear unstructured and jumpy. With the circle serving as the dominant center I can work abstractly with a quintessentially classic form while expanding my ongoing desire to explore new compositional possibilities. And even when it becomes overly fragmented and punctuated with other broken-edged clay forms the integrity of its circularity prevails.

*In life, it's up to you to choose what to emphasize.*

ANONYMOUS

There are numerous ways to intensify focal emphasis. For example, a repetitive series of textures or unremarkable forms commonly used to establish a pattern, institute proportional unity, or generate rhythmic harmony can be de-emphasized by the addition of a dissimilar form. This dissimilar form, whether it is of a different scale or a diverse energy, can resonate with emotion and serve as a visual catalyst to excite the viewer. By being at once radically different yet familiar within the framework of ceramic forms it becomes a dominant feature and a center of interest. Similarly, designs of all kinds can be given embellished areas of visual interest by altering the scale of a key feature or by simply jazzing it up in such a way that it contrasts with the colors, shapes, and/or surface textures surrounding it.

*Congratulate yourselves if you have done something*
*strange and extravagant and broken the*
*monotony of a decorous age.*

RALPH WALDO EMERSON

Only we can see into the creative uniqueness of what our clay work is about and by honoring that uniqueness find the specific solutions that each work requires. If we are having organizational difficulties with our designs we may need to search for deeper clarity within ourselves to discover not only what matters for our work but also how best to interpret and convey our insights through designs that reveal them to the viewer. Once we've internalized what it is we want to express through clay and have a more insightful understanding of our personal freedom of self-determination we are at liberty to make creative decisions that take our work beyond the status quo.

*An artist chooses his subject . . .*
*that is the way he praises.*

FRIEDRICH NIETZSCHE

By claiming this inner power we transcend circumstances that might have in the past limited our creative thoughts, feelings, and energies. With a greater acceptance of self we immediately recognize our ability to change our designs for the better. As this acceptance grows the power within us grows. No longer do we have to rely on forces outside of our selves. Whenever we see that a design isn't working, rather than turning to a marketplace of conventions we can connect to an inner strength that reveals the impact each and every design element and principle has on the overall aura of the work. If, for example, a design is lacking emphasis we can introduce the necessary changes to navigate it towards a successful outcome— one that resonates with the energy of our convictions and celebrates the creative miracles that are centered within us.

*Great things are not done by impulse, but by*
*a series of small things brought together.*

VINCENT VAN GOGH

Louise Nevelson once said, "Greatness breaks laws." The same is true with great artists and great designers—they too break laws. Their breakthroughs come from breaking from prevailing landmarks of convention. As they search through their personal sense of self and reconfigure their awareness, distinctions between self and designing break down, opening the way to other more fascinating modes of existence and an expansive generation of new rules. By subjecting a design to the scrutiny of our inner self or spirit is to give it the breath of life and fresh emphasis.

# 21

# Placement

*Designs of purely arbitrary nature cannot be expected to last long.*

KENZO TANGE

The placement of a clay object's individual elements is crucial to the visual quality of its composition. The relationships between the various parts that make up the whole of the work not only emphasize its visual cohesiveness, they also comprise an essential part of its aesthetic identity. It is therefore vital to have a comprehensive understanding of the dynamics of placement since it is essential not only to the successful correlation of compositional parts but also to the overall visual character of the work itself.

*Everything is expressed through relationships.*

PIET MONDRAIAN

I was once told that if at first sight a work of art could hold a person's attention for longer than eight seconds it was a commendable piece. Many years later a stranger attending an exhibition of my work told me that a praiseworthy sculpture was one that appeared significantly different from eight or more vantage points. Whether these two theories or the recurrence of the number eight has any connection to the viewing experience is open for discussion. What is clear, however, is that the interest the work attracts and how the artist evokes that interest in the viewer is highly pertinent.

The personal visual response that a viewer has to a work of art can be characterized by two perceptual reactions, both of which are important to the relationship between the viewer and the piece. The initial reaction if it is overwhelmingly positive grabs the viewer's focus, attracting all of her or his aesthetic attention before anything else. The second reaction is one of absorption. At this point the work is so alluring that the viewer becomes viscerally charged, identifying with its aesthetic sensibilities and possibly desiring to possess or acquire it.

*The work of art must seize upon you, wrap you up in itself and carry you away. It is the means by which the artist conveys his passion. It is the current which he puts forth which sweeps you along in his passion.*

PIERRE-AUGUSTE RENOIR

In light of these observations how do ceramists generate heightened viewer response and sustained interest? The answer is through design. Just as design is the art it is also the answer and in this instance the visual principle of placement is what most sustains the

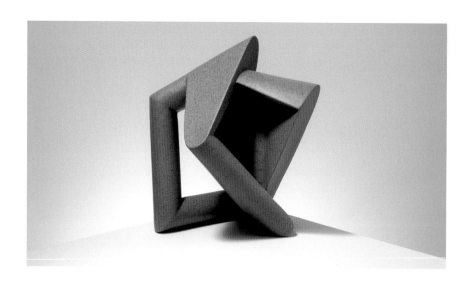

Anne Currier, *Swizzeld (4 views)*

quality of the work and captures the attention of the viewer. The substance of ceramic form depends on the arrangement of its various elements so placement is everything. Through the placement of parts the whole is made attractive to the viewer or undesirable, exciting or insipid, interesting or uninspiring.

Placement is the poetry of design. It is charged with uniting all of the elements into a visual expression of conceptual wholeness that translates into art and initiates acceptance. This is by no means an easy task. It calls for all kinds of personal skills but most importantly it calls on those specific qualities that universally define the artmaking phenomena of creative thinking and creative problem solving.

The designer, artist, or craftsman is someone who, in finding his or her own creative center is in touch with a sense of self and a higher caliber of thinking. This heightened level of thought processing goes by many names such as *critical thinking, imaginative thinking, artistic thinking,* and *intimate intuition*, but the term *creative thinking* is the standard label and the one most people equate it with.

*The truly creative mind in any field is no more*
*than this: a human creature born abnormally,*
*inhumanly sensitive. To them . . . a touch is a blow,*
*a sound is a noise, a misfortune is a tragedy, a joy is an*
*ecstasy, a friend is a lover, a lover is a god,*
*and failure is death.*

PEARL S. BUCK

This is a very powerful way of thinking and it is extremely useful for managing situations of uncertainty where a number of unknowns exist. Unlike a rational thought process, a creative approach generates multiple resolutions—some unique, some traditional. It's also a highly complex form of thinking in that it can simultaneously view events and/or criteria from many angles and even in the midst of confusion it can define structure and identify meaning.

When we are working the clay we are also working our minds. Creating is not an effortless process. It continuously finds us making all sorts of mental assessments and decisions based upon our own, not someone else's, accepted wisdom. Being creative is about more than originality. It's also about seeing and doing things in ways that others may have overlooked and having faith and courage in our own reasoning as we undertake new directions.

*Work out of your work.*
*Don't work out of anybody else's work.*

RICHARD SERRA

Individuals identified as creative thinkers and doers tend to be independent, spontaneous, uninhibited, and intuitively spiritual. They generally recognize the spiritual dimensions of self in their personal lives and have no problem letting the unseen energy of spirit be a co-creative force in their artistic lives. As the truest essence of who we are our spirit transforms our thinking and strengthens our will so that as ceramists we have to let it touch our work and contribute to the fullness of our designs. Each clay composition that we approach and seek to resolve presents us with a multitude of urges, questions, and visions that leave us searching for defining links and answers that often lie hidden in the shadows of our consciousness. The creative challenge for the designer is to locate the missing essentials and by using every means at their disposal introduce them into the clay composition via the spatial ingenuity of placement and the related components of scale and proportion.

> *Don't wait for what you need—put in the energy*
> *to create what you need.*

DAVID OLESKI

It's far too easy to work in clay and not know exactly what makes a work "art." The work itself holds the answer and by work I don't mean workaholic work where the physical pursuit is more important than the art. The work I am referring to is the finished artwork. It alone can signify that it is art. Apart from any personal ambition such as the desire for recognition, prosperity, expression, or other forms of fulfillment it is the design of the work that gives it an independent identity and ultimately answers for its worth.

Taken as a whole the compositional use of placement is the force that brings visual resolution to clay work. No other design element or design principle surpasses the principle of placement. Used mindfully and unaffectedly it strengthens the compositional artistry of the form and while touching the sensitivity of our spirit it captures the heart.

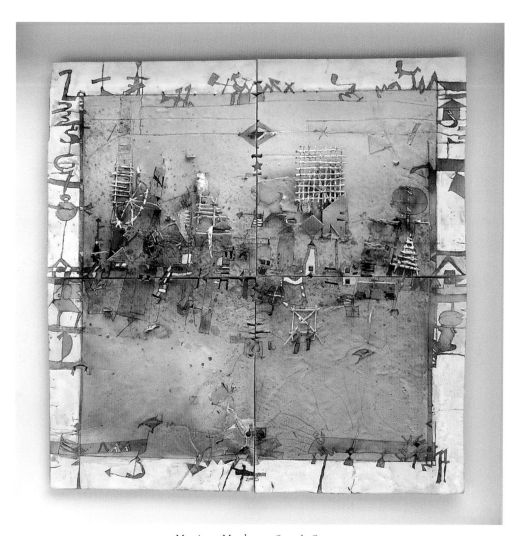

Monique Muylaert, *Over de Grenzen*

22

# Mystery

*The job of the artist is always to deepen the mystery.*

FRANCIS BACON

Mystery is the genesis of inquiry. With feelings of anticipation and adventure it beckons us forward into the unknown.

A month ago my wife and I made a trip to the mystifying city of Venice. Art is certainly plentiful there but in "our" Venice so is the ambiance: the faded colors, the historical emanation, filtered mists and floating objects bobbing up and down in the water—water absolutely everywhere. It is easy to become disoriented in Venice but there are times and places in life where being completely lost is desirable. This is a captivating city and we take a wanderer's delight in exploring the narrative of the unfamiliar via that mystery tour that leads us through canals, alleyways, and meandering streets with the fascinated hope of unexpected discovery. It is this very same sense of mystery that grabs our attention and holds our interest throughout the reading of a book, the performance of a play, or the viewing of an enigmatic work of art.

Gifted designers like insightful poets know how to invoke the veiled expectancy of undiscovered realities. Utilizing the elements of design they are able to subtly underscore the strengths and possibilities of the work in such a way that the power of the viewer's imagination is called upon for its completion. A good design like a good poem is respectful of others. By giving others the opportunity to be emotionally involved it acknowledges their ability to bring a part of themselves to the experience, thereby contributing to the work's significance. The impact of what is suggested or intentionally understated is far more important to the value of our designs than what is immediately visible. The same is true in our lives; there is no mystery or no magic in that which is overly stated and easily perceived.

*What's really interesting is the mystery. . . . seek mystery,*
*evoke mystery, plant a garden in which strange plants*
*grow and mysteries bloom. The need for mystery is*
*greater than the need for an answer.*

KEN KESEY

Mystery cannot be understood by the intellect or the senses alone. It is a presence. And as a presence it transcends the conventional complexities of usefulness. Like the nature of the universe or the nature of the self it is best approached within the context of spirit. Both spirit and mystery are invisible yet each has the potential to touch our lives and generate creative action while leaving us without a rational way to describe or define their reality. The cause-effect relationship in play here is itself a mystery. Salvador Dali claimed that people loved his paintings because they love mystery. It is, however, equally possible for us to utilize the creative potential of mystery in our work with clay even though we may not be entirely able to account for its illusory essence.

To avoid the certainty and predictability that comes from doing things in conventional ways it is important that we acknowledge our spirituality and believe in ourselves as creative beings. To bring mystery to our designs and excite the imagination of the viewer we have to trust these aspects of self and rely on our intuitive nature for faith and guidance.

*In the deep, unwritten wisdom of life there are many*
*things to be learned that cannot be taught.*
*We never know them by hearing them spoken, but we*
*grow into them by experience and recognize*
*them through understanding.*

ANTHONY HOPE

In its simplest sense, intuition is our natural ability for understanding the nature of things before assimilating similar perceptions through the knowledge of experience. It is instinctive knowledge and as such it comes through our spirit. Analysis and reason contribute little if anything to the insightfulness of intuitive comprehension. The basic truths of this unseen knowingness are what designers use to open expressive pathways for the unfolding presence of mystery. Mystery is everywhere waiting for an invitation to bring enchantment into our lives. As designers of clay we have

Peter Powning, *Arch Reliquary*

to realize that we are more than a pair of hands. We are spiritual beings with inner visions of creativity that reverberate from deep within. By tapping into our inner resources our work can be transformed with more truth and purpose than our conscious mind can fathom.

*Good design begins with honesty, asks tough questions,*
*comes from collaboration and from*
*trusting your intuition.*

FREEMAN THOMAS

When making major design decisions or even minor ones (which often turn out to be major ones) it helps if we surrender to the directional flow of our spirit and go with the unconscious wisdom of what presents itself rather than hold on to expectations. Within the creative flow between our spirit and intuition, mystery becomes possible. Our only mistake would be in responding too rationally as the process progresses. Like life, design has to occasionally depart from the rational and merge with the spirit of the unconscious if it is to have meaning.

At this point it's helpful to reflect on tradition and the function of trust. If we want our clay work to carry forward an energy of mystery and possess a measure of intrigue that is both captivating and uncontrived we either have to break with tradition or as many artists are doing expand on tradition. In either case style doesn't matter here. Our personal approach to clay can be as a sculptor (figurative or nonfigurative) or as a potter (functional or nonfunctional), but that has no relevance to whether or not the work expresses a natural quality of mystery.

A work of clay whether in the form of a teapot or an abstract sculpture can be visually safe and possess all the expected design components and still be boring, spiritually strained, and aesthetically stagnant. Expectations, like traditions, often inhibit the emergence of mystery and can eliminate the element of surprise and the unexpected. By staying within bonds they miss new possibilities.

I'm not saying we should oppose hundreds of years of ceramic traditions. I am saying that we should move past their limitations towards the more playful challenges of discovery. There is an infinite number of unseen design possibilities contained within each piece of clay. Each grants us opportunities to manipulate the medium outside the normal standards of shape formation so why not seize the moment and do the unexpected: enlighten the work by trusting in the mystery of our own aesthetic.

*I don't know of any good work of art*
*that doesn't have a mystery.*

HENRY MOORE

Mystery is imbued with multiple layers of meaning. The unrestrained designs of a perceptive ceramist can expose a new response, a richer vision, and most of all an alteration of form. To rise above the rules of convention and liberate our designs we have to have trust, and like our sense of design our trust is inherently intuitive: we ourselves define it. No one else can dictate, cultivate, or express it for us. We teach it to ourselves—no one can teach it to us. We are the only ones who can manifest our designs and infuse them with mystery. All of this takes place in the presence of trust. Without it our designs become overly contrived and self-conscious. In order to avoid artificial designs and provide our work with an unexpected

Nina Hole, *Honeycomb*

element of wonder we have to continuously surprise ourselves and not be spiritually complacent.

*The most beautiful thing we can experience is the mysterious. It is the source of all true art and science.*

ALBERT EINSTEIN

Learning reveals many things in life but there is no real understanding of mystery and its ability to awaken a design that can be objectified and artistically franchised as a paradigm of art education. As with designing, the workings of mystery cannot be easily explained, taught, or learned because they operate within us. Lacking an external reality and point of reference it exists as a personal expression of trust.

The essence of our designs is alive within us as the content and voice of our creativeness. Through self-trust we have the natural ability to supply whatever is needed to manifest them.

For the designer trust is a requisite. It empowers us to pass through the unknown and emerge with new and different ways of approaching our clay. Trust leads us to our intrinsic wisdom. With it we're in charge. We have the freedom to recalibrate our own process and attempt new ways of seeing that are more useful to our creative life than thinking itself. In the end our ability to traverse life's mysteries and to creatively process their emergent properties is what designing is all about. The question remaining is whether we do it with the essence of our spirit.

*Afterword*

Designing is one of my greatest joys. It allows me to be loving with myself—to surrender to my feelings and to bond with the simpler virtues of my spirit. As a visual artist I enjoy the creative achievements as well as the process. I enjoy the silent peace it brings and remain humbly grateful for both the personal and professional fulfillment it has bestowed upon me.

But right now as I write these closing words I take extra delight in having been able to share them, and most notably I feel grateful to you for having taken the time to read them. As Ralph Waldo Emerson said: " . . . the profit of books is according to the sensibility of the reader; the profoundest thought or passion sleeps as in a mine, until it is discovered by an equal mind and heart." My hope, despite the diverse nature of our individual spirits, is that we've attained moments of informed union and that our appreciation for the true significance of design as it enhances the holistic quality of our lives continues to grow. It is also with a hopeful sense of satisfaction that I've shared the valuable portfolio of photographs seen on these pages. They were the result of an extensive and international search of ceramic art. I trust you'll agree that the images chosen are an inspirational representation of both the human spirit and the art of design that is alive in the world of clay today. For these beautiful visual gifts their generous creators have my ongoing gratitude, reminding me once again of what Seneca advocated when he said: "We should give as we would receive, cheerfully, quickly and without hesitation, for there is no grace in a benefit that sticks to the fingers."

As ceramists and as human beings who understand the emotive values of giving we need to cheerfully and without hesitation expand upon our design skills by utilizing the personally expressive gifts of spirit to not only aid our constructions but to empower them as well.

Robert Piepenburg, *Toledo*

*A designer knows he has achieved perfection not when there is nothing left to add, but when there is nothing left to take away.*

ANTOINE DE SAINT-EXUPERY

# Contributing Artists

15    Enric Mestre, *Untitled*
      6.5 x 6 x 8 in. (16 x 15 x 20 cm)
      Groged stoneware and polished aluminum
      Photo by Manolo Artero
      E-mail: mestreestelles@yahoo.es

17    David Roberts, *Eroded Vessel*
      10.5 x 20.5 in. (27 x 52 cm)
      Naked raku fired coiled porcelain utilizing latex masking
      Photo by artist
      E-mail:  david@davidroberts-ceramics.com
      Website:  www.davidroberts-ceramics.com

23    Gennady Roitich, *Container for Important Word*
      9.5 x 21 x 10 in. (24 x 54 x 25 cm)
      Stoneware with copper oxide, iron salt and glaze
      Photo by Ilan Amihai
      E-mail: roitich@bezeqint.net
      Website: www.gennadyroitich.com

24    Paul Davis, *Slab Form*
      8 x 8 x 12 in. (20 x 20 x 30 cm)
      Wood fired Kagero clay and rice straw ash glaze
      Photo by artist
      E-mail: pdavis@hinet.net.au

29    John Brickels, *Buick Barn*
      24 x 13 x 9 in. (61 x 33 x 23 cm)
      Cone 3 stoneware
      Photo by Peter Wolf
      E-mail: guybarn@usa.net
      Website: www.brickels.com

33    Margaret Boozer, *Red Dirt Rake Print #2*
      8 x 10 x 0.5 in. (20 x 25 x 1 cm)
      Cone 6 earthenware print from a dirt drawing
      Photo by artist
      E-mail: margaret@margaretboozer.com
      Website: www.margaretboozer.com

36    Jim Kraft, *Log Jam #3*
       17.5 x 34 x 9 in. (44 x 86 x 23 cm)
       Earthware clay and glazes
       Photo by Richard Nicol
       E-mail: jimakraft@cablespeed.com

40    Craig Underhill, *Sun on Horizon*
       5.5 x 4.5 x 4 in. (14 x 11 x 10 cm)
       Low-fire clay, engobes, glaze and incised lines
       Photo by Martin Avery
       E-mail: craigunderhill@waitrose.com
       Website: www.studiopottery.co.uk

45    Monique Muylaert, *Ruimte III*
       25.5 x 25.5 in. (65 x 65 cm)
       Porcelain clay, multi-fired oxides and glazes
       Photo courtesy of Muys & Muylaert
       E-mail: info@artworks.be
       Website: www.artworks.be

47    Timothy Ludwig, *Lidded Jar with Crown Imperial*
       17 x 21 x 9 in. (43 x 53 x 23 cm)
       Low-fired red earthenware and slip with stains
       Photo by Randall Smith
       E-mail: taludwig@bellsouth.net
       Website: www.timludwigpottery.com

55    Ken Eastman, *Nova*
       16 x 14.5 x 16 in. (41 x 37 x 40 cm)
       White stoneware clay with colored slips and oxides
       Photo by artist
       E-mail: keneastman@btopenworld.com
       Website: www.keneastman.co.uk

58    Chris Staley, *Alchemy Still Life*
       15 x 22 x 9 in. (38 x 56 x 23 cm)
       Black clay wire cut and thrown stoneware
       Photo by artist
       E-mail: cxs41@email.psu.edu
       Website: www.sova.psu.edu

63  Elizabeth MacDonald, *Untitled*
    4 x 6 x 3 in. (10 x 15 x 8 cm)
    Low-fire clay, raw color pigments and acrylic
    Photo by Nathaniel Caronsky
    E-mail: elizabeth@elizabethmacdonald.com
    Website: www.elizabethmacdonald.com

66  Steven Hill, *Pitcher*
    17.5 x 8 in. (44 x 20 cm)
    White stoneware single-fired to cone 10
    Photo by Robert Piepenburg
    E-mail: gallery@centerstreetclay.com
    Website: www.stevenhill.com

69  Matt Wilt, *Server*
    14 x 13 x 10 in. (35 x 33 x 25 cm)
    Cast and thrown stoneware, concrete and steel
    Photo by Jon Koch
    E-mail: mwilt@siue.edu
    Website: www.siue.edu/ART

72  Velimir Vukicevic, *White Pitcher*
    6 x 5.5 in. (15 x 14 cm)
    Porcelain, latex on bisque, and sprayed with porcelain
    Photo by artist
    E-mail: vvukicevic@sbb.co.yu

75  Meredith Knapp Brickell, *Double Catch*
    8 x 29 x 9 in. (20 x 74 x 23 cm)
    Red earthenware with terra sigillata and glaze
    Photo by Lynn Ruck
    E-mail: meredith@mbrickell.com
    Website: www.mbrickell.com

77  John Herbon, *Untitled*
    6 x 6 x 6 in. (15 x 15 x 15 cm)
    White stoneware oxidation fired to cone 9
    Photo by John Wooden
    E-mail: johnherbonpottery@hotmail.com
    Website: www.johnherbonpottery.com

80   Margaret Boozer, *Red Fracture/Fill*
     23 x 23 x 1 in. (58 x 58 x 3 cm)
     Wet clay pressed into crushed red clay and fired to cone 6
     Photo by artist
     E-mail: margaret@margaretboozer.com
     Website: www.margaretboozer.com

83   Herman Muys, *Koning En Koningin*
     14 x 27.5 in. (35 x 70 cm)
     Low-fire clay, multi-fired oxides and glazes
     Photo courtesy of Muys & Muylaert
     E-mail: info@artworks.be
     Website: www.artworks.be

87   Gail Piepenburg, *Reflection*
     24 x 18 x 4 in. (61 x 46 x 10 cm)
     Raku fired with crackle glaze over stains
     Photo by artist
     E-mail: gailpotter@hotmail.com
     Website: www.piepenburgstudios.com

90   Matt Long, *Belly Button Cups*
     4 x 3.25 in. (10 x 8 cm)
     Porcelain soda fired to cone 11
     Photo by artist
     Website: www.fullvictory.com

96   Shozo Michikawa, *Square Incense Burner, Kohiki*
     4.5 x 4 in. (11 x 10 cm)
     Raku with silver lid
     Photo by Yoshinori Seguch
     E-mail: tobosho@nyc.odn.ne.jp
     Website: www.shozo-michikawa.jp/

99   Sam Chung, *Teapot*
     7 x 9 x 5 in. (18 x 23 x 13 cm)
     Soda fired porcelain
     Photo by artist
     E-mail: sam.chung@asu.edu

107 Nina Hole, *Boat*
15x 23.5 x 5.5 in. (38 x 60 x14 cm)
Low-fire oxidation
Photo by Ole Akhoj
E-mail: nihomi@getznet.dk
Website: www.ninahole.com

108 Anthony Caro, *Summit Games*
44 x 28 x 25.5 in. (110.5 x 71 x 65 cm)
Stoneware and steel
Photo by John Riddy
E-mail: sculpture@barfordsculptures.org
Website: www.anthonycaro.org

112 Lorna Meaden, *Watering Can*
13 x 14 x 6 in. (33 x 36 x 15 cm)
Soda fired porcelain with mishima decoration
Photo by artist
E-mail: lmmeaden@yahoo.com

115 Frank Saliani, *Analogous Radial*
26 x 21 x 7 in. (66 x 53 x18 cm)
Colored cast porcelain, wax and paint
Photo by artist
E-mail: fsaliani@yahoo.com
Website: www.franksaliani.com

116 Velimir Vukicevic, *The Plate*
20 in. (50 cm)
Thrown porcelain sprayed with slips over latex masking
Photo by artist
E-mail: vvukicevic@sbb.co.yu
Website: www.velimirvukicevic.com

119 L. Molnar Zsuzsanna, *I Live In You*
13 x 15 x 5 in. (33 x 37 x 13 cm)
High-fired chamotted clay with matt glazes
Photo by artist
E-mail: normallzsuzsi@freemail.hu

120　Kenneth Baskin, *Connections*
　　　13 x 24 x 13 in. (33 x 61 x 33 cm)
　　　Soda fired stoneware with slips and steel
　　　Photo by artist
　　　E-mail: kbaskin@mcneese.edu
　　　Website: www.kennethbaskinsculpture.com

128　Rudy Autio, *Apple*
　　　37 x 29 x 18 in. (94 x 73 x 46 cm)
　　　Slab-built stoneware with underglaze and cone 03 glazes
　　　Photo by Chris Autio
　　　E-mail: rautio@montana.com
　　　Website: www.rudyautio.com

131　Gail Piepenburg, *Suns of Sabone*
　　　9 x 11 x 3 in. (23 x 28 x 8 cm)
　　　Raku fired with crackle glaze over stains
　　　Photo by artist
　　　E-mail: gailpotter@hotmail.com
　　　Website: www.piepenburgstudios.com

133　David Roberts, *Large Vessel With Lines*
　　　21 x 19 in. (53 x 48 cm)
　　　Coiled porcelain raku fired with sacrificial resist slip
　　　Photo by artist
　　　E-mail: david@davidroberts-ceramics.com
　　　Website: www.davidroberts-ceramics.com

139　Kenneth Baskin, *Union*
　　　11 x 14 x 7 in. (28 x 35 x 18 cm)
　　　Soda fired stoneware with crater glaze and steel
　　　Photo by artist
　　　E-mail: baskinsouth@hotmail.com
　　　Website: www.kennethbaskinsculpture.com

141     Herman Muys, *Untitled Container #47*
        4 x 4 in. (10 x 10 cm)
        Low-fire clay, multi-fired oxides and glazes
        Photo courtesy of Muys & Muylaert
        E-mail:  info@artworks.be
        Website:  www.artworks.be

143     Chris Staley, *Stoneware Still Life*
        21 x 20 in. (53 x 51 cm)
        Wire cut and thrown stoneware
        Photo by artist
        E-mail: cxs41@email.psu.edu
        Website: www.sova.psu.edu

146     Brad Schwieger, *White Construction*
        18 x 7 x6 in. (46 x 18 x 15 cm)
        Salt fired stoneware with white slip
        Photo by Steve Paszt
        E-mail: bradschwieger@yahoo.com
        Website: www.ohio.edu/art

149     Robert L. Wood, *Twin Span*
        21 x 24 x 5 in. (53 x 61 x 26 cm)
        Low-fire earthenware clay with copper and steel
        Photo by artist
        E-mail:  woodrl@buffalostate.edu
        Website:  www.robertlwood.com

151     Fong Choo, *Tangerina*
        5.5 x 5 x 5 in. (14 x 13 x 13 cm)
        Thrown porcelain glaze fired to cone 6
        Photo by Bob Payne
        E-mail: fongc@bellarmine.edu
        Website: www.fongchoo.com

156 Robert Piepenburg, *Cyrex*
31.5 x 16 x 7.5 in. (80 x 41 x 19 cm)
Raku fired with under-fired crackle glaze
Photo by artist
E-mail: piepenburg@gmail.com
Website: www.piepenburgstudios.com

159 Joe Pinkelman, *Untitled*
30 x 15 x 15 in. (76 x 38 x 38 cm)
Decals on low fired clay and glaze
Photo by artist
E-mail: joepinkelman@yahoo.com
Website: www.joepinkelman.com

163 Elizabeth Lurie, *White on White Teapot*
7 x 7 x 7 in. (18 x 18 x 18 cm)
Porcelain with applied slip texture/pattern
Photo by artist
Website: www.elizabethlurie.com

164 Tom Phardel, *Union of Two Points*
13 x 24 in. (33 x61 cm)
Salt fired with crackle Avery slip
Photo by Artist
E-mail:  phardel@att.net

167 Meira Mathison, *Cruets and Tray*
4 x 4 x 6 in. (10 x 10 x 15 cm)
Reduction fired porcelain with slip and multiple glazes
Photo by Janet Dwyer
E-mail: mathm@telus.net
Website: www.missa.ca.

171 Gudrun Klix, *Porcelain Coracle III*
4.5 x 10.5 in. (11 x 27 cm)
Porcelain polished with wet and dry sand papers
Photo by artist
E-mail: g.klix@sca.usyd.edu.au
Website: www.freelandgallery.com.au/gudrun_klix.php

173 Maria Eitle-Vozar, *Card House WI*
Each around 8 x 5 x 6 in. (20 x 10 x 15cm)
High-fired porcelain with engobe and mixed media
Photo by artist
E-mail:  maria.eitle-vozar@bluewin.ch
Website:  www.maria-eitle-vozar.com

175 Daniel Evans, *Gratuitously Much*
48 x 25 x 19 in. (122 x 63 x 48 cm)
High-fire clay and Higby porcelain slip
Photo by artist
E-mail: abfclaydan@yahoo.com
Website: www.danielbrianevans.com

180-1 Gudrun Klix, *Night Journey*
11.5 x 33.5 x 7.5 in. (29 x 85 x 19 cm)
Earthenware ship with slip cast porcelain moon
Photo by Blue Murder
E-mail: g.klix@sca.usyd.edu.au
Website: www. freelandgallery.com.au/gudrun_klix.php

183 Margaret Boozer, *In Your Own Backyard*
70 x 30 x 6 in. (178 x 76 x 15 cm)
Steel, mastic and red earthenware fired to cone 6
Photo by artist
E-mail:  margaret@margaretboozer.com
Website:  www.margaretboozer.com

188-9 Jayson Lawfer, *Translation of an Important Idea*
4 x 14 x 5 in. (10 x 36 x 13 cm)
Terracotta and soda fired porcelain
Photo by Chris Autio
E-mail: jaylawfer@hotmail.com
Website: www.thenevicaproject.com

193 Jim Lutomski, *Winged Bottle Form*
16 x 16 x 6 in. (41 x 41 x15 cm)
Reduction fired stoneware with multiple glazes
Photo by Artist
E-mail: jlutomski@marygrove.edu.
Website: www.marygrove.edu

196-7    Eva Hild, *Working in the studio*
         Coiled forms twice fired to 1200°-1240° C
         Photo by artist
         E-mail: 2hild@bornet.net
         Website: www.2hild.com

201      Eva Hild, *Loop 785*
         27.5 x 31.5 x 27.5 in. (70 x 80 x 70 cm)
         White stoneware with kaolin engobe and silicate color
         Photo by artist
         E-mail: 2hild@bornet.net
         Website: www.2hild.com

204      Benjamin Carter, *Juice Glasses on Tray*
         4 x 14 x 14 in. (10 x 36 x 36 cm)
         Reduction fired thrown and altered porcelain
         Photo by Tom Mills
         E-mail: sp1r1tual@yahoo.com
         Website: www.carterpottery.com

209      Anthony Caro, *The Moroccans*
         72 x 80 x 68 in. (183 x 203 x 172.5 cm)
         Stoneware and earthenware with steel support
         Photo by Shigeo Anzai
         E-mail: sculpture@barfordsculptures.org
         Website: www.anthonycaro.org

212      Joe Szutz, *Myth of Invincibility*
         21 x 20 x 5 in. (53 x 51 x 13 cm)
         Low fired earthenware with slips and stains
         Photo by Mike Noa
         E-mail: jszutz@hotmail.com
         Website: www.joeszutzart.com

215      Herman Muys, *Troon*
         27.5 in. (70 cm)
         Low-fire clay, multi-fired oxides and glazes
         Photo courtesy of Melissa Muys
         E-mail: info@artworks.be
         Website: www.artworks.be

218  Ana England, *Touching the Earth*
     8 x 37 x 34 in. (20 x 94 x 87 cm)
     Photo by artist
     Burnished naked raku and carved porcelain
     E-mail: england@nku.edu

224-5  Anne Currier, *Swizzeld (4 views)*
       12 x 11.5 x 8.5 in. (30 x 28 x 22 cm)
       White stoneware glaze-fired to cone 03 and 08
       Photo by artist
       E-mail: curriera@alfred.edu

229  Monique Muylaert, *Over de Grenzen*
     27.5 x 27.5 in. (70 x 70 cm)
     Porcelain clay, multi-fired oxides and glazes
     Photo courtesy of Melissa Muys
     E-mail: info@artworks.be
     Website: www.artworks.be

233  Peter Powning, *Arch Reliquary*
     14.5 x 11 x 6 in. (37 x 28 x 15 cm)
     Raku fired clay, cast bronze and slumped glass
     Photo by artist
     E-mail: peter@powning.com
     Website: www.powning.com

236  Nina Hole, *Honeycomb*
     30 x 17 x 10 in. (77 x 44 x25 cm)
     Low-fire oxidation
     Photo by Ole Akhoj
     E-mail: nihomi@getznet.dk
     Website: www.ninahole.com

240  Robert Piepenburg, *Toledo*
     21 x 16 x 11 in. (53 x 41 x 28 cm)
     Low-fire oxidation
     Photo by artist
     E-mail: piepenburg@gmail.com
     Website: www.piepenburgstudios.com